THE U  ER

# THE **URBAN WILDLIFE GARDENER**

how to attract bees, birds, butterflies, and more

**emma hardy**

**CICO BOOKS**
LONDON  NEW YORK

This edition published in 2020
by CICO Books
An imprint of Ryland Peters & Small Ltd
20–21 Jockey's Fields    341 E 116th St
London WC1R 4BW    New York, NY 10029

www.rylandpeters.com

10 9 8 7 6 5 4 3 2 1

First published in 2015.

A CIP catalog record for this book is
available from the Library of Congress
and the British Library.

ISBN: 978-1-78249-819-3

Printed in China

Editor: Vanessa Daubney
Design concept: Geoff Borin
Designer: Sarah Rock
Photography: see page 144

Managing editor: Gillian Haslam
In-house designer: Fahema Khanam
Art director: Sally Powell
Production controller: David Hearn
Publishing manager: Penny Craig
Publisher: Cindy Richards

# Contents

# Introduction

With bees, butterflies, hedgehogs, and wildflower meadows in decline, it is more important than ever to garden with an awareness of our surroundings and consideration for ecological issues. Doing our bit is vitally important. In fact, wildlife that is struggling to survive in the wild can actually be well provided for in our gardens and backyards, so we should see it as our duty to help.

Creating the right conditions to attract a range of wildlife is relatively easy, rewarding, and fun to do, and will also help to produce a beautiful garden that you can enjoy. You don't even need a large garden—as this book will show, even the smallest urban garden or city balcony can be designed and planted to benefit wildlife.

Wildlife gardening does not mean that you have to let your whole garden become overgrown and unkempt, or that you need large swathes of ground in order to help wildlife. Devoting small areas to wildflowers and creating nesting sites and shelter can easily fit into even the most formal of gardens, or balconies and even window boxes. No matter what size your garden, it is easy to encourage a wide range of wildlife, and in this book you'll find plenty of ideas, lots of advice, and several projects to help you on your way.

# Getting started

Before starting, decide what you would like to attract and think about the practicalities. Obviously, you are unlikely to tempt hedgehogs onto your fourth-floor balcony, but you can increase the number of bees, butterflies, and moths very easily. Use this book to find specific plants, to help you plan your borders, and to get inspiration for longer term planting.

Looking around your neighborhood before planting will help. See what grows naturally in the wild, in hedgerows, on waste land, and also in the gardens surrounding your home. This will guide you toward plants that thrive in your area and which should flourish in your own garden.

Providing as many habitats as possible is an important part of a lively garden, so growing a range of shrubs and trees, creating log piles and other areas for shelter and possible nesting are crucial. In addition, adding a birdhouse like the green-roofed birdhouse on page 69, a bug hotel, such as the one on page 70, or a bee box (see page 83) will all help wildlife.

A garden that is rich in natural food supplies, with flowering plants, berries, seeds, and plenty of insects, can be enhanced by supplying extra food regularly, adding feeding stations, such as the pretty pinecone feeder on page 73 and the pumpkin feeder on page 76, and providing a range of foods for birds and small mammals. Information on suitable foods can be found in Chapter 5.

# Relax!

Gardening with a more relaxed attitude helps to increase wildlife, so let wild areas develop. Doing less pruning, tidying up, and plant maintenance, especially when it comes to trees and shrubs, won't hurt you and insects and birds will thank you for it. It will also give you more time to watch the wildlife that comes into your garden.

Creating a self-sustaining garden; collecting and using rainwater; employing organic principles by making natural fertilizers and pest controls; using companion planting; and planting for wildlife will all help to develop a truly stunning outside space, whatever its size.

I hope this book will inspire you to create your own wildlife garden, and that you will benefit from the joys of having wildlife on your own doorstep. You will not only gain enjoyment, but you'll also be helping nature, wildlife, and the environment.

OPPOSITE *There are many ways to encourage wildlife into your neighborhood. Growing a few trees and hedges is a great way to bring a variety of birds into your garden and will look attractive, too.*

BELOW *Placing a few birdhouses around your garden is so simple and will help to give valuable shelter and nesting sites for birds.*

# CHAPTER ONE

# Garden features

Whether you have a large, established garden with trees, hedges, and sweeping borders, or are new to gardening and eager to use every bit of space on your balcony or roof terrace, you need to consider the features that you have, or would like to include, in your garden. By adding a few extra elements to your garden and leaving some areas to become a little wilder, you can increase the wildlife activity in it quite substantially.

If you are making a new garden and are starting with a blank canvas, you can decide exactly what features you want, bearing in mind the particular wildlife that you would love to support, and plan accordingly. To attract more bees, butterflies, birds, and mammals into an existing garden, creating bug hotels, providing feeding stations, and introducing more flowering plants may be what is needed (see Chapters 5 and 7).

# Assessing your garden

*Some features of a garden will really encourage wildlife and help to create a self-sustaining plot. You may not want to include all of them, or indeed have the space, but choosing carefully and deciding what would fit in the space you have, be it a large, spacious garden or a tiny roof terrace or yard, will serve you well.*

## Drawing a plan

Draw a plan of your garden and note the sunny areas and those that may be in shade for much of the day, so that you can plan accordingly. Also note existing features so that it can act as a helpful reminder as to what you have in the garden already.

When planning where to plant borders, position a pond, or site feeding stations, it is important to think about the conditions that they will require. Pollen- and nectar-rich flowering plants usually require a very sunny spot; log piles and leaf piles need more shaded areas; while feeding stations demand various sites.

LEFT *An open, sunny area offers the perfect conditions for a variety of flowering plants, including lavender, foxgloves, nasturtiums, and even runner beans, all attracting bees, wasps, and butterflies.*

# Hard landscaping

**Walls and fences** Walls and fences are often forgotten spaces in a garden, but vertical gardening can unlock a whole new area of your garden that you hadn't considered before. You may already have climbers scrambling up walls, but hanging containers or pots on walls offer more planting opportunities, increasing the number of flowering plants, foliage, and even fruit and vegetables that you can grow. For recommendations on which climbers to choose, see Chapter 6, and for more information on vertical planting, see pages 12 and 94–97.

**Paved and decked areas** An area of paving or decking is often lacking in appeal to wildlife, but this is easily remedied. Adding pots of nectar- and pollen-rich flowers and herbs instantly provides interest for insects, birds, and mammals, while a mini pond is a source of water for wildlife and could encourage a few amphibians into your plot.

Concrete and paved areas do not absorb rainwater, and offer little support to wildlife, so if your garden or yard contains a lot of paving, consider removing some paving stones or some of the concrete to plant flowers, a few shrubs, or even a mini wildflower meadow.

**Lawns** A lawn can bring many benefits to the garden, but it is often not worth cultivating one in a small garden because maintaining it can be more trouble than it's worth. Consider turning it into a wildflower meadow, or allowing the grass to grow long, rather than trying to keep on top of a pristine and manicured lawn that offers little value to wildlife and which requires weekly mowing.

**Pond or bog garden** If you have an established pond already, then think about adding wildlife-friendly plants and features, planting in and around the pond to enhance its appeal. If your garden does not have a pond and it is not possible to build one, then why not try to find room for a mini pond in a tub, or a bog garden. See Chapter 4 for more information.

ABOVE *Growing climbers and shrubs up boundary walls and fences creates more opportunities for adding plants to the garden, helps to disguise the hard landscaping, and is beneficial to wildlife. Here, a tall sunflower will provide seeds for birds in fall and winter.*

## Soft landscaping

Trees are a wonderful addition to a garden and will attract a wide range of wildlife. Many gardens may not have room for large trees, but consider choosing a small variety, suitable for a container or patio area. It bring the same benefits without the need for acres of space. If you have trees in your garden already, then think about adding birdhouses and providing additional food to enhance their appeal to birds and bugs and help to create a haven for them outside your door.

Planting Planting shrubs and hedges helps to divide up spaces as well as provide shelter, nesting sites, and food, but if you really can't squeeze any into your garden then even a few pots bursting with flowering plants will bring interest for wildlife and are suitable for small spaces. For further information on trees, hedges, and shrubs, see Chapters 3 and 6.

Vertical planting Vertical planting has become very popular in recent years, and there is now a lot of expensive equipment and complicated watering systems available to buy in stores and garden centers. But making your own simple structures on a small scale can create more scope for growing plants and encourage wildlife when space is at a premium.

LEFT *A lovely vertical planter adds interest for wildlife in even the smallest of spaces, such as a balcony or roof terrace. Staple plastic sheeting around the back and sides of an old wooden pallet, fill it with potting compost, and plant it with a selection of heathers.*

## MAKING A HERB RACK

A wall is an ideal place to hang pretty, painted buckets filled with flowers or herbs to attract insects, and a herb rack is easy to make. These buckets contain a selection of herbs, including thyme, mint, chives, marjoram, and trailing nasturtiums.

1 Fix some lengths of galvanized wire horizontally to a wall. Place them about 12in (30cm) apart. Make small drainage holes in the base of each bucket.

2 Soak the root balls of the plants in water for 10 minutes or so before planting.

3 Add water-retaining granules to some potting compost (they will help to keep the plants moist, as they will quickly dry out in hot weather).

4 Place a little potting compost in each bucket and plant the herbs in them, filling any spaces with additional potting compost. Water well and remember to water on a regular basis, especially when the weather is warm.

5 Tie the buckets onto the wires with garden twine to hang them up.

# Green roofs

Green roofs fit very well into a garden designed to use every available space to the full. In a small garden or outside space, they can provide aesthetic benefits as well as ecological ones. A green roof on a shed, bicycle store, tool shed, summerhouse, or garden office can add greenery to an area that would otherwise look very dull.

Additional benefits include:
• Offering extra planting space, and by choosing your plants carefully (see panel on right) you can attract more wildlife to your garden.
• Water absorption, which in flood-prone areas can be very helpful, but be wary of the additional weight that water can add.
• Prolonging the life of a roof (if constructed properly) by preventing weather damage.
• Providing insulation, which on a shed used for work or storage is very useful.

In fact there are so many benefits to making a green roof, why would you not want one?

Before constructing your green roof, you must check that the structure of the building is strong enough to support the additional weight of the roof. If necessary, add extra supports inside the shed or out-house by fixing battens diagonally across the wall panels to strengthen them and ensure that they will not bow when the roof is in situ. For larger buildings, such as a garage or garden office, always consult a structural engineer for expert advice before starting work.

ABOVE *Give your garden shed, which is usually an uninteresting area of the garden, an extra dimension by making a green roof for it and thus an extra habitat for wildlife.*

# Plants suitable for a green roof

When choosing plants for your green roof, include evergreens and flowering plants because they will benefit wildlife throughout the year. Low-growing plants are a good idea because they are less susceptible to wind damage, and drought-tolerant plants are especially useful because watering the roof in hot weather may not be easy. Bear in mind whether your shed is in full sun or shade, too, although Sedum and Saxifraga tend to be as tough as old boots and will happily grow wherever you put them.

Try some of the following:

**Ferns**: such as Maidenhair Spleenwort (*Asplenium trichomanes*).

**Saxifraga**: these delightful little plants are ideal for roofs and there are many to choose from. *Saxifraga cuneifolia* (known as Lesser London Pride or Shield-leaved Saxifrage) is lovely, providing pollen and nectar for bees and butterflies.

**Sedums**: like Saxifraga, these make great covering plants for roofs. You can buy Sedum matting from good garden centers and simply roll it out onto the roof, providing a pretty mixture of plants that will appeal to many insects and birds. Or you can select individual sedum plants: *Sedum spathulifolium, S. rupestre, S. pluricaule,* and *S. acre* are all suitable, but there are many others to choose from.

**Thrift or Sea Pink** (*Armeria maritima*): very pretty and will tolerate dry conditions well.

**Wildflowers** (general): you can buy packets of mixed wildflower seeds and sprinkle them onto the compost, although they will obviously take longer to establish.

**Bulbs**: especially dwarf varieties, work well on a green roof. Try crocus, grape hyacinths (*Muscari*), and daffodils (*Narcissus*).

ABOVE *Even small structures can have a green roof. This version is covered in various sedum species and sits well on the top of a bug hotel, providing an additional level of shelter for nesting insects.*

# TO MAKE A GREEN ROOF

Buy water-retentive matting from specialist garden centers or via the Internet. The matting will prevent the roof from drying out and help to regulate moisture. Old woolen blankets can also be used as a cheap alternative, but they will rot down eventually. NB: The exact measurements of the wood that you need to make the frame of the green roof will depend on the size of the roof that you are covering.

## YOU WILL NEED

2 lengths of 8 x 1in (20 x 2.5cm) treated timber cut to the same length as the width of the roof

2 lengths of 8 x 1in (20 x 2.5cm) treated timber cut to the same depth of the roof minus 2in (5cm)

4 wooden battens (2 x 2in/ 5 x 5cm) 8in (20cm) long

2 lengths of 4 x 1in (10 x 2.5cm) treated timber cut to the same length as the depth of the frame

3 lengths of 4 x 1in (10 x 2.5cm) treated timber to fit between these central supports

1 piece of butyl liner (the size should be equivalent to the roof area with an additional 4in (10cm) or more (it will depend on the roof's construction) all round to overhang the edge of the roof)

1 piece of water-retentive matting (the size should be equivalent to the roof area with an additional 6in (15cm) all round to overhang the roof)

L-shaped brackets

Nails and/or screws to fix the timber together

Alternative to the timber listed above: a piece of plywood cut to the dimensions of the roof

1 Join together the first two longer lengths of timber and the second two shorter lengths to form a rectangle (or square, depending on the dimensions).

2 Screw one of the four battens at each corner, so that they stand vertically, to hold the frame together. The two shorter lengths should sit inside the longer pieces.

3 Place the two lengths of 4 x 1in (10 x 2.5cm) treated timber cut to the same length as the depth of the frame equidistant from each other across the inside of the frame to form a central support structure. Screw them in place from the outside of the frame at either end.

4 Place the remaining three lengths of timber between these central supports to form a grid. Fix them in place using metal L-shaped brackets, screwing them together securely. This will help to hold the soil and plants in place.

5 Cover the roof with the butyl liner and tack or staple it in place along the edges of the roof, making sure that you fold it neatly at the corners. Then repeat with the water-retentive matting, fastening it in place in the same way.

6 Lift the frame into place on top of the roof, and drill a few large holes along the front edge to help drainage. To make sure that the frame is held securely in place, it is a good idea to add an additional batten along the front of the roof and screw it into both the shed and the frame.

7 Mix together potting compost and perlite (which will lighten the soil) in equal parts. Cover the drainage holes with a few pebbles before you fill the frame with potting compost, so that they will not get blocked up.

8 Fill the frame with the compost and perlite mixture. You are now ready to start planting (see page 15 for suitable plants).

Alternative method: Cut a piece of plywood to the exact dimensions of the roof. Cover it with the butyl liner and then the water-retentive matting, folding the liner and the matting underneath the plywood and tacking or stapling them in place. This will provide extra protection for the shed roof, and is a good idea if your shed is a few years old. Place the plywood on top of the shed and secure it in place with wooden battens along the front and back edges.

## Wild areas

Leaving your garden or backyard to "go wild" will help visiting wildlife enormously, and so finding a small area or two for grass to grow tall, for leaves to gather and rot down, or for logs and garden debris to collect are important in a wildlife-friendly garden. However, your garden does not need to become completely overgrown and unkempt—by choosing and planning carefully, you will be able to maintain a beautiful garden that provides benefits for all.

## Seating areas

Areas for secluded seating are vital in your garden. Having cultivated and encouraged a wildlife-friendly space, quietly sitting down to observe the comings and goings of the many and varied visitors to your garden will be your deserved reward. A few seats dotted around your garden will allow you to enjoy different views of your space from various angles, and at different times of the day and evening. At the very least, try to squeeze in a small seat or bench on which to relax with a cup of coffee and take the chance to marvel at nature on your doorstep.

ABOVE *Create spaces in your garden to relax and enjoy watching the wildlife. Shady areas provide the perfect spot for a bit of birdwatching, especially if you site feeding stations and nesting areas nearby. Remember that you may need to sit very still so that your wildlife visitors are not disturbed.*

# CHAPTER TWO

# General housekeeping
## *in the* garden

A wildlife-friendly garden creates valuable habitats
for all sorts of creatures with the added bonus of
requiring less maintenance than a more formal space.
It is the perfect opportunity to be lazy in the garden and
let nature take its hold. The idea of leaving seed heads
in place and letting the lawn grow tall may go against
traditional gardening methods, but it is vital in a garden
that wants to encourage wildlife to visit and settle.
Leaving parts of the garden to grow a little wilder and
creating areas of logs and twigs will give ideal shelter
for wildlife and help to build a self-sustaining habitat
that can also offer food, water, and nesting sites.

Even a well-tended garden can sustain a certain
amount of wildlife, but it is relatively easy to entice
even more species without letting your garden become
completely wild. Choosing small areas and setting up
wildlife-friendly projects are very rewarding and will
increase the visitors to your garden enormously.
You may find that you enjoy the benefits of
a wilder garden so much that you decide to
devote even more space to it.

# Garden organically

*The wildlife garden welcomes a wide range of insects and invertebrates in to it, but there are a few that are perhaps less desirable than others.*

Anyone who has had their precious seedlings savaged by slugs, or their dahlia blooms decimated by earwigs, will have been tempted to attack the problem with chemicals, but knowing the effects of these treatments should make us look at alternative approaches that will be much less harmful to the environment.

## Reasons to avoid pesticides

Nurturing your garden, perhaps taking a more tolerant approach and being happy to co-exist a bit more with all our wonderful wildlife, will create a happier, healthier environment. Using pesticides has a knock-on effect in various ways:

● Blasting infestations of aphids with chemical sprays may well rid your plants of the problem, but can harm ladybugs that feed on aphids and reduce their numbers in your garden as they look elsewhere for food.
● Sprinkling slug pellets around your seedlings may prevent their attacks, but the pellets can harm hedgehogs and birds who consume the poisoned slugs.
● Using any chemicals in the garden will have a detrimental effect on the surrounding area and upset the natural balance of the environment. All the creatures in your garden have a use: in their turn, they provide food and nourishment for other creatures, so banning chemical pesticides, herbicides, and insecticides is really the most sensible approach.

ABOVE *Young seedlings need protecting from predators. Avoid using chemicals and employ more natural repellents (see pages 22–23) for a healthier and more ecologically sound garden.*

## MAKE YOUR OWN INSECT REPELLENT

**Garlic spray is an effective insect repellent and can be made easily from general household ingredients.**

1 Crush a bulb of garlic and mix it with approximately 2 pints (1 liter) of water in a large saucepan.

2 Heat the water until boiling and then turn the heat off and leave the mixture to cool.

3 Add 1 tablespoon of natural soap (available from health food stores), which will help the liquid stick to plant leaves, to the liquid and pour it into a jar. Label the jar and keep in the fridge.

4 To use the mixture, fill a spray-top bottle with water and add 1 tablespoon of the garlic liquid. Spray it on plants and the surrounding soil to repel insects. Repeat the process every few days to help keep the bugs at bay.

## Peat-free potting compost

Peat bogs have been in serious decline over recent years, mainly because of the overuse of peat in horticultural products. This has serious consequences for wildlife because the bogs are home to many rare insects, birds, and plants, and they need to be protected to prevent further damage. The farming of peat bogs also releases carbon dioxide, which is detrimental to the environment. Used for its moisture-retentive qualities, peat now has several effective replacements, so there really is no need to use it. The alternatives on the market will do the job just as well.

Bearing this in mind, using peat-free products is a must in the garden, especially when it comes to potting mediums. These are widely available from garden centers, but it is worth checking the packaging just to make sure that they are completely peat-free.

# Preventing pests

Rather than resorting to chemical pesticides and insecticides, try to tackle the problems organically. There are many natural solutions to unwanted pests that will not cause harm to plants, animals, or the garden as a whole.

- Looking after the soil is a fundamental way of controlling pests because the healthier the soil, the healthier the plants will be, making them more resilient to infestations and attacks.
- Adding mulches of compost and enriching the soil with well-rotted manure will provide the best start for plants and help them to grow strong.
- Companion planting is a great way of deterring unwanted visitors and can be highly effective (see pages 118–125).
- Cutting the bases off plastic bottles and placing them over young plants (remove the lids first) can protect them from slugs, snails, and insects.
- Implementing some of the following solutions (or several of them at once if necessary) will help in the battle against the bugs:

## Caterpillars

- Check plants regularly, and pick the caterpillars off. Put them on the bird table to feed our feathered friends.

BELOW *Slugs can decimate seedlings and young plants, but there are several ways of discouraging them, including making protective cloches from plastic bottles (bottom).*

## Earwigs

- Place upturned plant pots (terracotta pots are best because plastic ones are a bit lightweight) on garden canes stuck in the ground around the plants, with a handful of straw in each one. Earwigs seek out dark corners to hide in and will gather in the pots. Shake the pots out each morning to remove the earwigs and this will allow your flowers to bloom.
- Spray plants with liquid seaweed (available from good garden centers and on-line stores).

## Greenfly and black fly

- Grow marigolds because they do not like the smell.
- Spray plants with liquid seaweed.
- Spray diluted nettle feed (see page 27) onto plants.

## Lily beetles

- Check plants regularly, removing the eggs, grubs, and beetles as and when you find them.

## Slugs

- Encourage hedgehogs, frogs, and toads into the garden.
- Place prickly plants like thistles around plants.
- Sprinkle crushed eggshells around plants (slugs do not like the rough texture).
- Put copper tape round the top of plant pots because it gives slugs small electric shocks and they will not cross it.
- Bury beakers of beer or milk in the soil near plants—slugs are attracted to the smell and will fall into the liquid and drown.
- Place rhubarb leaves round plants. They attract slugs, which will gather underneath and you can then dispose of them.

## Vine weevils

- Check plants regularly, particularly at night, and pick the weevils off. If you can, take plants out of containers to check the soil for the grubs or beetles.
- Sit container plants in large saucers of water—vine weevil beetles cannot fly or swim, so will not be able to get to the plants.
- Encourage birds, hedgehogs, toads, and newts into the garden.
- Add a thick layer of gritty sand around plants to prevent the weevils from laying eggs.

ABOVE *Ladybugs will feast on aphids, helping to keep their numbers down without the need for chemicals.*

# Letting go

*With wildlife gardening, the general rule is the less intervention the better. Tempting though it may be to cut back and tidy plants and flowers at the end of the growing season, it is better for wildlife to leave things be and, in their own way, seed heads and dying flowers can look quite beautiful. Delaying pruning and deadheading will add to the appeal of your garden to wildlife.*

ABOVE *While it is important to leave dead flower heads in place over winter, deadheading during the flowering season will keep plants in bloom longer, providing pollen and nectar for insects for more of the growing season.*

**Deadheading:** holding back on deadheading will provide the perfect habitat for insects like ladybugs and lacewings over winter, as well as ground cover for small mammals and amphibians. The frost-covered, dried stems and flower heads of sedum (*Sedum* var.), penstemons (*Penstemon* var.), and eryngiums (*Eryngium* var.) allow insects to nest and birds to feed as well as providing beauty and form in a flower border over winter.

**Tidying up:** if you would rather cut back your borders at the end of summer, maybe to make way for new plants or bulbs, or simply to tidy up, consider leaving intact just one or two plants that have gone over to provide a bit of shelter and food. Tidy shrubs and borders that have been left in the spring so that they will have been of benefit throughout the winter, and keep the cuttings for the compost heap.

**Pruning:** Climbing plants often provide shelter and food for birds and insects, so it is important to prune them at the right time. It is generally recommended that climbers are cut back after flowering at the end of summer, but leaving them until early the following spring will provide shelter (and food if they have seeds and berries) and ensure that nesting sites have been vacated. Dense climbers are more likely to attract nesting birds, so try not to thin the plants out too much when pruning, although cutting off diseased or overcrowded branches will help to keep the plant in good shape, so there does need to be a healthy balance. Not all climbers will need to be pruned every year, so leaving some to spread and grow tall can bring benefits to even more wildlife.

# Weeds *for* wildlife

*The term "weed" is usually used when talking about plants that are unwanted in the garden. They may be invasive, unattractive, and undesirable, but in a wildlife garden weeds can be considered friends because they benefit many insects, providing food for butterfly caterpillars, nectar for bees, and seeds and berries for birds.*

## Weed maintenance

You may not want to cultivate weeds throughout your borders and pots, but setting aside a small area can provide many of the benefits without letting them take over. Although many weeds can be invasive, regular maintenance in the garden should keep them in check and prevent them from spreading too far. A small square at the edge of a flower border or a patch of lawn out of view from the house will do, bearing in mind that the sunnier a spot, the more butterflies will be attracted to it.

## A weed garden

**1** To create a weed garden, simply leave the ground un-weeded and un-mown and in no time a range of weeds will have sprouted up, benefiting a whole host of wildlife.
**2** Check around the weed garden regularly, pulling up any stray weeds from the surrounding area to keep them under control and stop them from spreading.

RIGHT *Leave a few weeds or flowering plants to set seed and grow in your borders to increase the number of butterflies visiting your garden.*

# Nettles

Nettles are essential to many of our most loved butterflies, and so incorporating some into your garden is very worthwhile. They also provide shelter for overwintering insects and will attract aphids, which in turn will feed ladybugs.

**Containing nettles** These are not the prettiest of plants, and have the added disadvantage that they sting, so most gardeners avoid nettles and try to eradicate them from the garden, but siting them out of reach and containing them will give you all the benefits without the drawbacks.

Growing nettles in a pot means that they can be positioned in the middle of a flowerbed where they will be out of the way, and will not have the opportunity to spread across the garden. This is also a good idea for balconies and roof terraces where, if you position the pot in a sunny spot, the nettles will attract butterflies and encourage them to lay their eggs.

BELOW *Nettles are usually something to avoid in a garden, but they offer a lot of value to a wildlife garden, attracting many insects. Use them to make plant feed for the vegetable patch.*

## MAKING A NETTLE GARDEN

1 To make a nettle garden, fill a large plant pot with garden soil (or potting compost if that is not available).

2 Dig up nettles from your own garden or offer to dig up nettles or take seeds from friends' gardens (they'll love you for it!), and re-plant them in your pot. If your friends think you've gone mad, invite them round to watch the butterflies and moths gather and the nettles hum with life and maybe they will want one, too.

3 Cut back nettles in early summer to encourage a late flush that will benefit wildlife for even longer.

## Nettle feed

Another benefit of nettles is that they can be used to make a nitrogen-rich feed that is very useful in the garden. Collect nettles, either from your own garden or from any surrounding wasteland (make sure that you don't take too many wild nettles, because they benefit insects in the wild as well), and steep them in water to make a great plant feed that won't cost you a penny.

1 Cut down nettles, break them up a little (wearing protective gloves), and put them in a large bucket.

2 Cover the nettles with water, and put the bucket out of the way, preferably far from any seating areas and patios because it does get quite smelly!

3 Leave the infusion for approximately two weeks. Then strain the liquid off, chucking the soggy nettles onto the compost heap. Your nettle feed is now ready to use.

4 The liquid is very concentrated, so dilute it in a ratio of one part feed to ten parts water and it will not cause damage to plants.

5 This nettle feed is excellent for many plants, especially brassica and other leafy green vegetables. Avoid using it on seedlings and young plants because it will be too potent.

# Tree care

*If pruning or cutting down trees, keep the off-cuts for a log pile or to place under hedges. Leaving tree stumps in the ground will provide habitats for a number of invertebrates as the wood rots down.*

## Dead wood

Dead wood actually attracts more insect life than living wood. So making woodpiles—which are easy to create and which encourage many insects (especially beetles), as well as mosses, fungi, and lichens—is a must.

## Log piles

• Laying a few logs in a shady corner of the garden creates a cool, damp area. You can add more logs and twigs as appropriate.

• Growing honeysuckle or clematis over the log pile makes an attractive cover and also helps to retain moisture.

• Any insects that gather there will provide a feast for birds, especially baby birds because the insects enable them to grow and survive the winter.

• Damp, woody areas will also encourage lichen to grow, benefiting moth caterpillars and fungi that help to break down organic matter, providing perfect habitats for lots of wildlife.

LEFT *Building a log pile is a simple and effective way to create habitats for wildlife. Pile logs and twigs in a shady spot, pushing dead leaves and soil between them to encourage nesting insects and bugs.*

**Making a log pile** Dead and decaying wood is the perfect habitat for many plants, amphibians, mammals, insects, fungi, and lichen, and is easy to provide even in small gardens.

Your log pile may become a shelter for insects, such as ground and stag beetles, woodlice, earwigs, and wasps, as well as slugs, snails, frogs, toads, shrews, and wood mice. Many insects lay their eggs in log piles, and some, like the stag beetle eggs, may remain in one place for several years, so it is important not to move your log pile once it is up and running.

**1** Collect wood from tree pruning. Ask neighbors for some if your garden does not have trees in it, including twigs and branches as well. Never take wood from the wild, where it may already be benefiting wildlife.

**2** Find a shady spot so that the log pile will not dry out, preferably somewhere that will not be disturbed. Keep your log pile sited away from living trees because the dead and decaying wood may harbor harmful bacteria, which could damage healthy trees.

**3** Partially bury a few logs in the soil and then pile other logs, twigs, and broken branches on top, adding a few handfuls of soil and leaves as you go to help keep the mound moist.

**4** Make sure your log pile is not too tall, because this would make it harder to maintain the damp conditions, and also it could topple over.

ABOVE *Log piles offer homes to a variety of insects, including spiders. Invaluable in the garden, spiders are a great natural pest control, particularly in the battle against aphids.*

## MAKING A MINI LOG PILE FOR A BALCONY

**1** To create a woodpile on a small patio or balcony, simply partially bury logs around the base of plants in pots and planters. Add wood chippings if you can get hold of them. They can look decorative as well as be useful.

**2** Alternatively, take a pot or old bucket, add a few holes if it does not have any, and fill with soil and wood chippings, bits of bark, and small twigs. Finish by placing a few logs on the surface. This is not really a decorative feature, but it will sit happily behind other pots and plants.

# Leaves

*Allowing fallen leaves to stay on the ground creates a hibernation spot for hedgehogs as well as many insects and provides a natural mulch to help protect plants from harsh weather over winter. But if you have a lot of fallen leaves to deal with, then there are some things you need to consider.*

Raking a heavy fall of leaves from the lawn is a good idea because, left in situ, they can starve the grass of oxygen and weaken it. Plus, they can also play host to slugs and snails, which are often the more unwelcome guests in the garden, wildlife-friendly or not!

Leaf piles, however, are a great way of providing shelter and food for frogs, toads, hedgehogs, and lots of insects, and are so easy to make that it would be silly not to bother. Shovel fallen leaves under hedges and bushes, or behind plant pots and containers, where they will not be seen but will provide a useful service.

## Leaf mold

If the idea of letting leaves lie on the ground is a step too far, then gather them up into jute bags (available from garden centers) or plastic garden bags with a few holes in them. Water them well, and put to one side. In a year or so, you will be left with beautifully rich, crumbly leaf mold, which makes the perfect mulch and can be added to potting compost.

LEFT *Rake up piles of leaves in shady spots to provide shelter and food, or fill jute bags with them to make leaf mold.*

OPPOSITE *As summer fades, fall leaves introduce color and beauty into the garden and can have many uses for wildlife.*

## Making a stumpery

Popular with the Victorians, and present in many 19th-century gardens, stumperies were a practical alternative to rockeries, when large stones were unavailable. They were used to house and exhibit exotic collections of ferns and to create visual features in gardens, but they are a useful addition to a wildlife garden because, like a log pile, they support many species of insects, plants, mosses, and fungi. They have the added benefit of looking beautiful in the garden and will certainly create a talking point.

**1** To make a stumpery, find some large tree stumps, trunks, and branches. Driftwood works beautifully, too. It may be worth contacting local professional gardeners to source these.

**2** Position your stumpery in a shady spot to replicate woodland conditions where ferns, among other plants, will thrive.

**3** Dig a hole in the earth and arrange your wood, laying tree trunks on their side so that the roots can be seen, to make an attractive arrangement.

**4** Bury shorter logs and tree bark around these, covering and backfilling round them with a mixture of about 50 percent leaf mold and 50 percent topsoil.

**5** Place your plants around the wood, moving them until you are happy with the arrangement, and then plant them up, adding more soil if necessary. Water the stumpery well.

ABOVE *For a modern take on a traditional stumpery, arrange logs and tree off-cuts in a shady area and plant ferns among them, mimicking woodland conditions.*

### Plants suitable for a stumpery

**Ferns,** such as **Hart's Tongue** (*Asplenium scolopendrium*), **Japanese Shield fern** (*Dryopteris erythrosora*), **Maidenhair fern** (*Adiantum pedatum*)

**Hostas** (*Hosta* species)

**Hellebores** (*Helleborus* species)

**Primula** (*Primula* species)

**Sweet Woodruff** (*Galium odoratum*)

**Bishop's Hat** (*Epimedium* species)

# Compost heaps

*I am a firm believer that a garden is not complete without a compost heap, and this is especially true when creating a wildlife-friendly garden. As well as being a highly effective way of recycling your garden and kitchen waste and supplying you with copious amounts of precious compost and soil improver, a compost heap can host a wide range of insects, mammals, and even amphibians that will benefit your garden enormously.*

The process of composting may seem complicated, but once the heap is up and running, it is actually very easy and will reward you well. Compost bins are available to buy in varying shapes and sizes to suit any garden, or you can easily construct your own with wooden posts and chicken wire.

## Setting up the compost heap

Ideally, the compost heap should be positioned in a shady spot on bare earth to increase the insects and worm population, encourage micro-organisms, and help with drainage.

## What to compost

Pretty much all garden waste, apart from any diseased material, can be put on the heap, but bear in mind that very woody cuttings will take longer to rot down, so chopping them into smaller bits will help. Try to add a good mixture of waste as too much of any one thing may upset the natural balance.

- Grass cuttings can be put on the compost heap, spreading them out a little, and adding shredded or scrunched-up paper or cardboard with them so that the heap does not become too soggy.
- Leaves from nearby trees can be added, but can

ABOVE *Compost heaps do not have to be an eyesore. This pretty wooden compost bin, designed to look like a beehive and painted a soft gray-blue, is especially useful in a small garden where it may be hard to hide a compost heap.*

take a while to rot down. To speed up their decomposition, you can pile them on the lawn and mow over them with the lawnmower to chop them up. Alternatively, see the information of leaf mold (see page 30).

• Kitchen waste, such as vegetable and fruit scraps and peelings, teabags, coffee grounds, and eggshells are all ideal. Do not include meat or cooked food scraps since they can attract rats (see Wormeries, page 36).

• Even the contents of the vacuum cleaner can be added, which also helps to stop the heap becoming too wet.

## MAKING A COMPOST HEAP

1 Measure and mark out a square on the soil no smaller than 1 sq yd (1 sq m).

2 Take four wooden posts about 4½ft (1.5m) long and knock a post into each corner of the square. Make sure that they stand firmly upright in the ground and that their height is equal.

3 Take a roll of chicken wire (or similar) and fasten the edge to one of the posts using a heavy-duty staple gun or cable ties.

4 Wrap the chicken wire around three sides of the square, cutting it with wire cutters to the correct size, and attach the other edge to the last post in the same way as before, leaving the front open.

5 Staple or tie the chicken wire onto the back posts with cable ties to make the structure more secure.

## Moisture and decomposition

- Check the heap regularly to make sure that it is damp but not too wet (add newspaper or cardboard if it is, and water if it is very dry).
- Turning your compost heap is not absolutely necessary, but it can speed up decomposition. Using a garden fork, simply turn the contents of the heap over gently, checking to make sure that there are no small mammals, frogs, or toads resting in it.
- Nettles, comfrey, and even urine (I will leave this one up to you!) will all add nitrogen to the compost heap and thus speed up the composting process.
- Your compost heap should reward you with dark, crumbly, sweet-smelling compost after approximately six months. Use it as a soil conditioner, potting compost (sieve it first), or rich mulch.

## Insects and worms

A healthy compost heap will support a wide range of insects and bugs. Expect to see woodlice (which break down organic matter as they feed), brandling worms (which do a great job of turning the soil), beetles, and slugs (they may be unwelcome in other parts of the garden, but they feed on dead plant matter and provide food for hedgehogs and birds).

If you see large numbers of ants in the compost heap, it can be a sign that the matter is too dry, so add some water.

*ABOVE If you have the space, use several compost bins to ensure that all your garden waste is recycled, by adding fresh waste to one heap at a time, leaving the others to rot down more quickly.*

# Wormeries

*If you really don't have the space for a compost heap, then a wormery may suit you very well. They take up little space, are easy to look after, and are a very effective way of recycling kitchen waste.*

## Positioning a wormery

It is important that the worms do not get too hot or too cold, so place the wormery in a shaded spot and wrap either bubble wrap or old blankets round it during cold weather. This will ensure that the worms remain productive and happy.

Be aware that wormeries are unsuitable for most garden waste, but unlike a compost heap, you can add cooked food and meat, so they are very handy for a wildlife-friendly space no matter the size. Available from good garden centers and specialist suppliers, wormeries usually consist of two or three compartments with a tray and a faucet or tap at the bottom to collect the liquid waste, which is a wonderful fertilizer for plants.

## Setting up a wormery

**1** Place some coir or compost in the first (top) compartment. Then add the worms. Use brandling or red worms, which can be purchased with your wormery. Earthworms are not suitable for a wormery.
**2** Add a small amount of kitchen waste. You can gradually add more kitchen waste until the compartment is about two-thirds full. Selecting a wide range of kitchen waste is very important. Don't add onions, garlic, leeks, or citrus fruits because these will upset the worms and alter the pH balance too much.
**3** Once the first compartment is two-thirds full, move the next compartment to the top to repeat the process. The worms will work their way up through the layers, leaving rich composted material behind them that can be used as a soil improver or potting compost.

**Using wormery compost** Dig the wormery compost into the soil well when using it in the garden because it can form solid lumps that are difficult to break up if it dries out. The wormery also produces a constant supply of liquid fertilizer which is rich in nitrogen and potassium. Dilute it with water in a ratio of about one part fertilizer to ten parts water. I keep empty plastic bottles to store this in and use it weekly on containers and vegetable beds during the summer.

# Water supplies

*Rainwater is every gardener's friend. It is the best thing to use for watering plants, filling ponds, and maintaining healthy lawns. Building up reserves of water in water butts throughout the year will ensure that you can water the garden even in hot spells and times of drought.*

**Water butts** Available from garden centers in a range of shapes and sizes, from large plastic containers to neat metal tubs in a variety of colors, water butts or rain barrels are best sited underneath a down pipe, so that they will collect as much rain as possible from guttering. Shop-bought water butts usually feature a faucet or tap so that you can easily fill a watering can. Any watertight container or tub can be used to collect rainwater if you don't have access to a down pipe. In that case, it's advisable to attach some mesh over the top to prevent small mammals and birds falling into it.

**Gray water** During long, hot summers, it may not be possible to provide your whole garden with collected water. Using "gray water," that is water from washing dishes, baths, showers, and washing machines, can effectively keep the garden watered. Use gray water straight away because storing it may encourage bacteria to grow, but don't use it on salad crops or other food crops that will be eaten raw. Domestic soaps and detergents should not pose a problem, although using organic, chemical-free brands is advisable. Water that has been mixed with bleach or strong chemical cleaners should never be used in the garden as it will harm plants and wildlife.

There may well be times when using tap water is the only option, but with a little planning, it should be possible to maintain a healthy garden using collected and waste water only.

ABOVE *A water butt is a must in any garden. If possible, position one near the vegetable patch, which will need additional watering during dry spells.*

# CHAPTER THREE

# Trees, hedges, *and* lawns

Trees, hedges, and lawns are probably the three
largest elements in a garden and, if it is large enough,
your garden may well contain examples of all of them.
As with any planting for wildlife, you should aim for as
many varieties of these as you can, providing different
kinds of shelter, nesting sites, shade, and food, which,
in turn, will create a beautiful garden.

If you simply do not have room for large trees or
hedges and a lawn is not worth cultivating due to the
size of your garden or yard, then it is still possible to
include some of these elements, albeit on a smaller scale
and in a more controlled way. This chapter will give
you the information you need to establish and grow
trees and hedges and will also offer ideas for more
wildlife-friendly ways of cultivating lawns that can
be adapted in lots of ways to suit your garden,
whatever its size.

# Trees

*When thinking about ways to encourage wildlife into the garden, trees must come at the top of the list. They provide food, shelter, and nesting sites for birds as well as for lots of other species almost all year round. From buds and flowers in spring to fruits in summer, and berries from autumn onward, trees are the best and most comprehensive source of food for birds, plus they bring beauty, shade, and many ecological benefits to your garden.*

ABOVE *A berry-laden tree will feed a whole host of birds, providing them with valuable food as winter approaches.*

The oak (*Quercus*) is one of the most elegant and important species of tree. It supports hundreds of different types of wildlife—from birds such as tits, chaffinches, woodpeckers, and jays, to insects that include moths, butterflies, and beetles, as well as wood mice and squirrels. The bad news is that the oak is too large for most domestic gardens; the good news is that there are many more trees, including a number that are suitable for small spaces, that will fit in well and offer many resources to wildlife.

## Choosing a tree

If your garden has established trees in it already but you would like to plant more, or you are introducing trees onto your plot for the first time, you must think about the eventual height and spread of each tree, or you could end up with a tree that is far too large and which dominates your space.

Don't plant large trees too near the house, especially if you have clay soil, because trees absorb a lot of water which makes the soil shrink, potentially causing damage to the foundations of the house. Ask the nursery or garden center for advice before you buy a tree because different varieties of the same tree may grow to very different sizes so it is always better to check first to avoid problems in the future. When choosing a tree, look at natives that grow naturally where you live and are suited to the local conditions and support a wide range of wildlife.

# Ideal trees for a wildlife-friendly garden

**Common or European Ash** (*Fraxinus excelsior*) is only suitable for large gardens. Appeals to lots of insects and provides seeds for birds and small mammals.
Max height: Above 40ft (12m).
Max spread: Beyond 26ft (8m).

**Common Hawthorn or May** (*Crataegus monogyna*) produces red berries that appeal to thrushes, redwings, and fieldfares. Its flowers attract bees, and it is a great habitat for moth caterpillars and mammals nesting over winter.
Max height: 13–26ft (4–8m).
Max spread: 13–26ft (4–8m).

**Crab Apple** (*Malus sylvestris*) provides flowers for bees, is a good habitat for invertebrates, and produces fruit as food for birds and mammals.
Max height: 26–40ft (8–12m).
Max spread: 13–26ft (4–8m).

**Field Maple or Common Elder** (*Acer campestre*) attracts bees, wasps, and moth caterpillars, and produces fruit for small mammals.
Max height: Above 40ft (12m).
Max spread: 13–26ft (4–8m).

**Goat or Pussy Willow** (*Salix caprea*) produces catkins that provide pollen and nectar for insects. It also appeals to bees and moth caterpillars.
Max height: 26–40ft (8–12m).
Max spread: 13–26ft (4–8m).

**Hazel** (*Corylus avellana*) supplies nuts for birds, such as jays and woodpeckers, and mammals. It is also attractive to moth caterpillars.
Max height: 8–13ft (2.5–4m).
Max spread: 8–13ft (2.5–4m).

**Hornbeam** (*Carpinus betulus*) provides seeds for birds and nesting cover.
Max height: Above 40ft (12m).
Max spread: 13–26ft (4–8m).

**Rowan or Mountain Ash** (*Sorbus aucuparia*) appeals to blackbirds (which love the berries), starlings, redwings, fieldfares, aphids, sawflies, and other insects.
Max height: Above 40ft (12m).
Max spread: 13–26ft (4–8m).

**Silver Birch** (*Betula pendula*) provides food for hundreds of species of invertebrate, seeds for birds (such as finches and blue tits), catkins for redpolls and tits, and a habitat for moths, beetles, and sawflies. It is also a great haven for moth larvae.
Max height: Above 40ft (12m).
Max spread: Beyond 26ft (8m).

**Wild Cherry** (*Prunus avium*) provides pollen and nectar for bees from flowers, and its cherries feed birds.
Max height: Above 40ft (12m).
Max spread: Beyond 26ft (8m).

## Conifers

Many gardens or backyards have a conifer or two growing in them, and while they are not hugely beneficial to wildlife, they do offer year-round shelter and nesting sites for a variety of birds and small mammals. You may find tits, chaffinches, and sparrowhawks making their nests in them, or mice, voles, and even red squirrels, if you have them in your area, using them for shelter; while insects, including aphids, often gather on them, providing food for birds.

Planting new conifers may not be a priority in a wildlife-friendly garden, but recognizing the benefits that they do bring, and maybe hanging bird feeders on the branches or growing climbing shrubs up them to maximize these benefits, will help to justify their inclusion in the garden.

BELOW *A female sparrow surveys the area from its vantage point at the top of a conifer.*

# Hedges

*Hedges have many purposes in a garden or yard: marking and providing living boundaries, reducing noise pollution, creating wind-breaks, and adding valuable shelter and food for many birds, insects, and mammals.*

They offer varied interest all year round, creating nesting sites and shelter for birds and bees, which like to build their homes around the base and can also find hedges a source of nectar and pollen. Butterflies and moths especially like hedges with white and cream flowers, such as blackthorn; while birds, hedgehogs, and other mammals are attracted to the berries and seeds in winter.

## Existing hedges

Established hedges will already be supporting a wide range of wildlife, but assess their general health and wellbeing and consider their uses to wildlife to help you to decide how best to increase their value in the garden. You may need to add more hedging or replace diseased areas, or you may want to plant around the base of the hedge. It may just be a case of improving the overall state and look of the hedge through maintenance and pruning.

### Adding to an existing hedge A garden hedge can create
woodland conditions, which are a welcome addition to any garden. If you have hedges in your garden already, you can add plenty of things to enhance their appeal to wildlife.

• Birds need dense planting to provide areas for nesting, so filling in any gaps in the hedge by adding more plants helps to thicken the vegetation and offers shelter from predators. You might want to introduce different varieties to the hedge to appeal to a wider range of creatures.

• Planting woodland flowers and plants around the bottom of a hedge will increase the number of insects in and around it. Celandines (*Ranunculus ficaria*), primroses (*Primula vulgaris*), garlic mustard (*Alliaria petiolata*), and wood anemones (*Anemone*

ABOVE *Honeysuckle (*Lonicera *species), with its nectar-rich flowers, can be grown through evergreen hedges, creating more interest for wildlife, and helping to provide food and shelter for birds, insects, and small mammals.*

*nemorosa*) will look pretty and are also a good source of food for insects.

● To create more shelter and encourage bees among other species to nest under the hedge, let the grass grow underneath and around hedges, and put twigs, branches, and fallen leaves in and around the base.

● Growing climbers up a hedge will provide additional cover and attract pollinators to the flowers. Clematis (*Clematis* var.), honeysuckle (*Lonicera* var.), and ivy (*Hedera* var.) are all suitable and will feed birds with seed heads and berries, too.

BELOW *Leave hedges to become dense and prune them carefully to allow birds and insects to shelter in them and to provide year-round interest in the garden.*

# Planting a new hedge

If you decide to plant a hedge in your garden, perhaps to replace or disguise a dull fence or separate different areas, think about growing one made from several different plants to increase the appeal. Ideally, plant new hedges in the fall or autumn when the ground is not too waterlogged or frozen.

1 The best way to plant a hedge is to buy small plants known as whips, which—although they may take longer to establish than larger plants—will in time give a dense, even hedge.

2 Preparing the soil well is vital; the hedge will become a permanent fixture, so giving it the best start will help it to grow robust and strong.

3 Clear the area where the hedge will be sited and dig in plenty of compost or well-rotted manure. This will feed the plants and help to retain moisture during spring and summer, and prevent waterlogging, which is particularly important as the plants establish.

4 For a wide, dense hedge, planting in two rows is a good idea, but this will need a wider area. For a thinner hedge, which will not create such a dense environment, planting a single row will be fine and will still have lots of benefits. Dig a trench, adding a few handfuls of fertilizer, and position the plants between 12 and 15in (30–40cm) apart. If planting a double row, plant the second row 12–15in (30–40cm) away from the first, and stagger the plants in an alternate pattern. Backfill the trench around the plants, and firm the soil well. Water well and do not let the soil dry out.

5 It is a good idea to weed around the base of the hedge for the first year at least to allow the hedge to establish itself without struggling to access water and nutrients. Apply a mulch to the soil around the base of the hedge, and put twigs and leaves around the plants as well. This will help to prevent weeds growing, as well as encouraging wildlife.

## Ideal plants for wildlife-friendly hedges

**Beech** (*Fagus sylvatica*) gives year-round cover for birds. Produces nuts as food for finches and tits.

**Blackthorn** (*Prunus spinosa*) produces flowers that will benefit insects and offers good cover for birds.

**Common Buckthorn** (*Rhamnus cathartica*) produces berries for birds and mammals and flowers that attract butterflies and bees.

**Hawthorn** (*Crataegus monogyna*) is a great haven for many insects and birds, such as sparrows, wrens, thrushes, and blackbirds, by providing food and nesting sites. Its flowers are good for bees and the foliage appeals to moth caterpillars.

**Hazel** (*Corylus avellana*) is popular with insects, while the nuts provide food for birds and mammals.

**Holly** (*Ilex aquifolium*) produces red berries loved by starlings, thrushes, and fieldfare. It also attracts the holly blue butterfly.

**Hornbeam** (*Carpinus betulus*) attracts tits and finches, which adore the seeds, as well as small mammals and insects, especially moths.

**Spindle** (*Euonymus europeaeus*) produces fruit and seeds for birds, and is a popular home for insects.

# Looking after a hedge

While the desire for a neat hedge may be strong, it is important not to over-prune as that may have a detrimental effect on wildlife.

For new hedges, cut the growth back to about 20in (50cm) in the first spring after planting. This will encourage bushy growth and prevent the bushes from becoming too "leggy" (top heavy, with a spindly base).

Trim established hedges every other year so that you do not disturb too much wildlife. Cutting sections of the hedge (and leaving some areas unpruned) is also beneficial. Never cut hedges back during the mating season, between spring and late summer. Ideally, leave it until late winter, when birds will have had the opportunity to feast on berries and seeds and will no longer need their nesting sites.

# Dead hedging

If a living hedge is not possible, then why not create a dead hedge? The wildlife will love it and the great thing is that it is free. Dead hedging is a very simple way of creating a barrier and may well play host to amphibians, a variety of invertebrates, and small mammals, too.

### How to create a dead hedge
The idea is to weave and intertwine twigs, sticks, branches, and dead flower stalks around and between vertical wooden posts, which can be made to any height or depth. You will need some small tree trunks or thick branches to act as posts. The length can vary, depending on the height you want the hedge to be.

1 Knock the posts into the ground in a line so that they stand firmly upright. Position them about 16in (40cm) apart.
2 Add another line of posts 16in (40cm) apart from the first line, staggering them in an alternate pattern with the first set of posts.
3 Weave some of the longer woody prunings around the posts (this can be done quite roughly) and pile the other branches and flower stalks between the posts to build up the hedge.
4 As the dead hedge rots down (which you want it to do so that it creates similar conditions to a woodpile), simply add more prunings and flower stalks to build the hedge up again.

# Shrubs

*Introducing shrubs to your garden can add structure and form as well as provide beautiful flowers and foliage, fragrance, and in some cases year-round color.*

The term "shrub" covers a wide range of plants, from small, compact bushes to plants that are as tall as trees. Different varieties of the same species can vary greatly in size and shape, too, so it's important to consider the suitability and position of new shrubs. When choosing shrubs for the garden, bear in mind that some of them can reach great heights although, unlike trees, they can often be kept to size with careful pruning.

In a wildlife garden, in particular, shrubs can provide shelter and food for most if not all of the year, and will sustain a wide range of wildlife. Shrubs can serve as valuable nesting sites, evergreens being especially useful at times of the year when deciduous shrubs and trees are still in bud. For more information on shrubs, see Chapter 6.

RIGHT *Planting a range of shrubs in your garden will help wildlife all year round, and add color and texture to the garden throughout the seasons.*

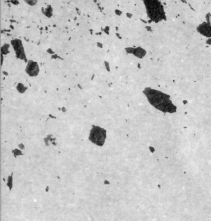

LEFT *If the idea of leaving your lawn to grow completely wild is a little too much, creating wilder planting areas around the edge of the lawn and allowing smaller areas of grass to grow longer will still bring many benefits for local wildlife.*

# Lawns *and* grassy areas

*Lawns, traditionally an important part of a formal garden, add a neat focal point, but letting them grow and encouraging wildflowers into them helps to create a haven for a wide range of insects which in turn provide food for birds and mammals.*

Providing space for recreation, a prime spot for a bit of sun worshipping, or the perfect place for al fresco dining, a well-manicured lawn is often much desired, but letting it grow wild can bring a new beauty to your garden with colorful cornflowers, chamomile, poppies, and ox-eye daisies popping up alongside delicate grasses to give a shimmering, soft elegance as well as offering a home to hundreds of bees, bugs, and butterflies.

Wildflower meadows are often associated with the countryside, but they can be created in small urban gardens and backyards, too. From a small area of an existing lawn to pretty much the whole garden, wildlife meadows can fit into any space and are often a more practical solution than a simple grass lawn in a small garden. Once they are established, they will require less maintenance, and you won't need to buy and store a lawnmower because meadows can be cut back with a sharp pair of shears. A wildflower meadow or patch can also be a very economical use of space, as it will provide beauty and many benefits to wildlife without the need for a large garden.

# Easy wildflower lawns

*The easiest way to create a wildflower lawn is simply to let the grass grow longer, allowing daisies, dandelions, and seeding grasses to thrive, perhaps mowing a path through the middle to create a beautifully soft and naturalistic effect.*

- Depending on how big your lawn is, why not mow a section in the middle of the meadow for a table and chairs, giving you the perfect place for dinner and a spot of wildlife-watching while you eat.
- If the idea of letting your whole lawn go wild is a little too daunting, then set aside a strip of grass and leave it un-mown to make a smaller, but equally effective, wildflower patch. Leaving grass to grow along shrub borders is particularly beneficial to invertebrates, which will in turn provide food for birds and hedgehogs, mice, and voles.
- Mowing your lawn to different lengths encourages a variety of insects by providing shelter for moths, butterflies, sawflies, and crane flies as well as their larvae in longer grass. Bees, moths, and hoverflies will love the nectar and pollen from flowering plants, and birds will enjoy the seeds that follow. An added benefit of longer grass is that it retains moisture and so will be less prone to drought in very hot weather.
- Leaving grass long over winter gives shelter to insects and provides a habitat for butterfly and moth caterpillars, beetles, grasshoppers, crickets, and spiders, and they in turn provide food for birds when it may be scarce in other areas.

RIGHT *Let your lawn grow to encourage a range of pretty wildflowers to seed and bloom. The result will be a beautiful meadow and the wildlife will enjoy it, too.*

# Creating a wildflower meadow

*Wildflower meadows look wonderful, but actually require some preparation and careful maintenance to achieve. Do not let this put you off, though, because the results will be well worth it.*

ABOVE *Choose native seed mixes when planting a wildflower meadow and buy them, rather than gathering them from the wild, because doing so may deprive the local area of native plants.*

OPPOSITE *Choose bulbs that will produce pollen- and nectar-rich flowers, such as narcissi and crocuses, to feed insects from late winter onward. Buy them from reputable nurseries or garden centers, making sure that the bulbs look healthy and have not dried out too much before planting.*

1 Wildflower meadows require relatively poor soil, otherwise grasses will take over and you will have fewer flowers. If you are planning to use ground that has previously been cultivated you will need to remove the topsoil or grass to a depth of about 4in (10cm).
2 Dig up any weeds, leave them lying for a few weeks, and clear the ground as other weeds appear. Dig over the soil and tread it down lightly, raking it to make an even surface.
3 Choose a seed mix that contains native plants and which suits your conditions well, and sprinkle it over the soil. Water the ground.
4 When the meadow has grown up, mow it three or four times in the first year to a height of about 2in (5cm), leaving the cuttings in place for a day or two to give the seeds a chance to fall. Then clear them away to prevent too many nutrients reaching the soil.
5 Leave the meadow over winter and mow it again in spring and then again in fall. Take time to enjoy the beautiful, ever-changing variety of flowers and grasses that grow, and give yourself some time to sit back and observe the vast array of wildlife that will flourish.

## Adding wildflowers to an existing lawn

If creating a meadow is not a suitable option, cheat a little and pop in some plugs of wildflowers to an existing lawn. It is a much simpler, but very effective, alternative.

Look for plant nurseries that specialize in wildflowers to buy plugs and matting. Wildflower matting is available from specialist nurseries, many of which sell their products online. It is similar to grass turf in that it will arrive in rolls and needs to be planted quickly to prevent it drying out, providing you with a "carpet" of wildflowers. It is an easy and effective way of creating a wildflower garden quickly. Choose native plants and species or varieties that grow well in local hedgerows and meadows around your neighborhood.

Dot the plugs randomly around the lawn or group them together in clusters. Dig holes the same size as the pots, remove the plants from the pots, and plant them without adding any potting compost or soil improver.

## Bulbs

Planting bulbs in the lawn creates a similar effect to adding plugs of wildflowers, and they will provide valuable nectar and pollen from late winter through to early spring—a time when these foodstuffs can be in short supply in the rest of the garden.

Narcissus (*Narcissus* var.), fritillaria (*Fritillaria meleagris*), grape hyacinth (*Muscari* var.), and crocus (*Crocus* var.) bulbs can be planted in the lawn in fall. To achieve a natural look, throw them randomly onto the grass and then plant them where they land. Cut a small square in the turf with a sharp knife, pull back the turf, and plant the bulbs at a depth of twice their height, then press the turf back down firmly.

Once the bulbs have flowered, let them die down before mowing the grass, so that the bulbs will conserve their energy and flower again the next year.

## A MINIATURE WILDFLOWER MEADOW

**If space really is at a premium, why not grow a miniature wildflower meadow in a container. It's perfect for a balcony or patio area.**

1 Choose a container with drainage holes in the bottom. Drill a few holes in the base if it does not have any.

2 Place a few broken pieces of plant pot (or coarse gravel) in the base of the pot to help with drainage.

3 Fill the pot with peat-free multipurpose potting compost or garden soil, and flatten the surface.

4 Sprinkle wildflower seeds over the potting compost or soil and press gently into the surface. Water well and position in a sunny site, and then just wait for the flowers to grow.

# CHAPTER FOUR

# Water features

Introducing water into your wildlife-friendly garden is probably one of the most important things you can do. A pond is a wonderful addition and attracts more wildlife than just about any other element. Expect to see dragonflies, damselflies, pond skaters, water beetles, frogs, newts, and toads, as well as a whole host of visiting birds, bees, and butterflies, and, if you are lucky, a hedgehog or two.

If your garden has enough room for a pond, then putting one in will provide plenty of opportunities for encouraging wildlife. With an established pond, you can add more beneficial plants and create areas for specific creatures. Even with a small outside space, water can still play an important role. Creating a bog garden or mini pond in a tub will bring many of the benefits of a pond, and they can be squeezed into the tiniest of balconies and terraces. A small birdbath will attract birds and insects and takes up very little room, but provides a very worthwhile service and will encourage more wildlife into your garden for you to enjoy.

# Pond features

*If you already have an established pond in your garden (lucky you!), then you may have had the pleasure of watching insects swooping and buzzing over the surface, or observed a greenfinch taking a dip or a submerged toad happily poking its head out of the water. But improving access to your pond and carrying out regular maintenance can increase the wildlife activity and help to keep the pond in good shape.*

Consider the following aspects. Ponds with shallow sides and a gentle slope give frogs, toads, birds, and hedgehogs access to the water without danger of drowning. If your pond does not have this, think about placing some bricks, stones, or upturned plant pots in and around the pond to create a slope out of the water. Cover them in hessian or burlap sacking or chicken wire if they are very smooth to give a little grip.

Creating areas of shallow water with submerged planting will encourage dragonfly and damselfly larvae, and frog tadpoles. Use some stones or gravel at the edge of the pond and add a branch or a large stone that breaks the surface of the water to act as a perch for birds and bees while they take a drink of water.

LEFT *Maintaining a healthy pond provides the optimum conditions for wildlife. Growing a few water-loving plants in and around the water will create the ideal environment for amphibians, insects, and birds.*

OPPOSITE *A frog sits happily on a lily pad.*

## Planting a pond

**1** When planting up a pond, or adding new plants, always use aquatic potting compost with a heavy loam content because it contains a slow-release fertilizer that will not pollute the water and will stay in place rather than float around the pond.

**2** Most aquatic plants are sold in mesh baskets, which help to keep potting compost and roots in place. If your plants are not in baskets, then it is well worth potting them up before planting them in the pond. You will be able to buy additional baskets from garden centers and aquatic stores.

**3** Fill a basket about two-thirds full of potting compost and place the plant onto it. Add more potting compost until it reaches just below the surface and water well, or submerge the container in a large bucket of water for several minutes.

**4** It is a good idea to cover the surface of the potting compost with gravel to help keep it in place.

**5** Lower the plant into the water, placing it in its final position. Make sure that it is not completely submerged (unless it is an oxygenator—see the plant list on the right). Place some bricks underneath the container, if necessary, to achieve the correct depth. Floating plants should sit on the surface of the water, marginals around the edge and in shallower water, and oxygenators should be planted in the deepest spots.

## Plants for ponds

Adding plants to a pond is the perfect opportunity to choose wildlife-friendly varieties. If you have a large pond, you can add marginals around the edge of the pond, with a selection of oxygenators and floating plants, too, but for smaller ponds consider the size and spread of the plants carefully because some can become quite invasive. Choose plants that suit the depth of your pond, checking their requirements before planting.

### Marginal plants
**Lesser Spearwort** (*Ranunculus flammula*)
**Marsh Marigold** (*Caltha palustris*)
**Water Forget-me-not** (*Myosotis scorpioides*)
**Lizard's Tail or Swamp Lily** (*Saururus cernuus*)
**Flowering Rush** (*Butomus umbellatus*)

### Submerged plants (oxygenators)
**Hornwort** (*Ceratophyllum demersum*)
**Starwort** (*Callitriche palustris*)
**Water Milfoil** (*Myriophyllum spicatum*)
**Water Crowfoot** (*Ranunculus aquatilis*)
**Water Violet** (*Hottonia palustris*)

### Floating plants
**Water Soldier** (*Stratiotes aloides*)
**Frogbit** (*Hydrocharis morsus-ranae*)
**Water Lettuce** (*Pistia stratiotes*)
**Water Velvet** (*Salvinia natans*)
**Floating Marsh Marigold** (*Caltha natans*)

## Planting around the pond

Planting around the pond creates habitats for insects and amphibians, and provides green corridors that allow easy movement between the pond and the garden. Iris are well suited for this, with *Iris laevigata* and *Iris pseudacorus* being particularly lovely (although the latter can be very invasive, so should not be planted in water courses). Zebra rush (*Scirpus zebrinus*) and Common Arrowhead (*Sagittaria sagittifolia*) also work well, and adding hostas and primulas, or even just leaving the grass to grow long around the water's edge, will all soften the look of the pond and help wildlife habitats.

Here are some other plants to consider:
**Arum Lily** (*Zantedeschia aethiopica*)
**Devil's Bit Scabious** (*Scabiosa succisa*)
**Fleabane** (*Pulicaria dysenterica*)
**Great Willowherb** (*Epilobium hirsutum*)
**Lady's Smock** (*Cardamine pratensis*)
**Ragged Robin** (*Lychnis flos-cuculi*)
**Salad Burnet** (*Sanguisorba minor*)
**Wild Angelica** (*Angelica sylvestris*)

## Safety near water

Pond safety is very important. If you have small children or they are likely to visit regularly or play in your garden, then it is vital to include safety measures to prevent accidents. Growing large plants around the pond will help to create a barrier, but think about adding a fence and installing a solid mesh cover for the pond to limit access to it. Alternatively, build a bog garden (see page 61) until the children are older—this will still entice lots of wildlife into the garden, but will be much safer to curious young children.

# Caring for your pond

**1** Don't keep fish in your pond if you want to attract frogs, toads, and a variety of insects, because the fish will eat many insects and thus make the water less attractive to other wildlife.

**2** Dead leaves can lower the oxygen levels in the water, so remove them from the pond regularly. Be ruthless with plants that grow a little too vigorously: divide them and throw some on the compost heap, but leave them by the pond for a day or two before doing so, so that any insects living in them can move back into the pond. Aim to have no more than half of the surface of the water covered.

**3** Ideally, your pond will be in a sunny spot. Cut back any overhanging foliage to let as much light and heat as possible get to the plants to keep them healthy.

**4** If the water becomes discolored with a green scum on the surface, there is too much algae, which thrives in warm, sunny spots and particularly when there is a lot of debris in the pond. It also reduces the amount of oxygen in the water. In that case, add an oxygenating plant (see page 55), or tie a handful of barley straw or lavender in a bundle and throw it in and it should clear it within a few days.

**5** Always top up your pond with rainwater because tap water contains chemicals that can upset the balance of the wildlife pond and encourage algae to develop. See page 37 for more information.

**6** Try to clear the pond in fall when there is less wildlife activity and possibly lots of dead leaves and dying foliage that need clearing away. This is also a good time to divide plants that have become too large for the pond. Continue to do this throughout winter.

**7** When the weather gets really cold, place a ball (such as a tennis ball, or something similar that will float) on the pond's surface to help prevent it from freezing over. If the surface of the water does freeze, break the ice regularly so that wildlife can still access the pond.

ABOVE *Keep an eye on the pond and clear away plants that become too invasive, removing any dead leaves to keep oxygen levels in the water up.*

# Making miniature ponds

*Even the smallest of spaces, such as a patio or balcony,
can benefit from a water feature, and it's easy to make
a mini pond in an old bathtub, sink, or half barrel.*

**1** Choose a container that is watertight and frostproof, and clean it thoroughly. I have had a mini pond in an old galvanized washing tub for several years and, despite its small size, it attracts many different insects and several toads, too. If your container is small, limit the number of plants that you put in it so that it will not become overrun with foliage.

**2** Find a sunny spot for your pond, to help to attract more wildlife.

**3** Add a layer of washed sand or potting compost to the bottom of the tub to allow insects to burrow.

**4** As with a large, permanent pond, your mini pond needs sloping sides to allow wildlife safe access to the water. Place some stones, bricks, or upturned plant pots in the tub to build up different levels, making sure that some of the stones or pots break the surface of the water.

**5** Ideally, fill the tub with rainwater (a water butt or rain barrel is handy for this) because tap water contains chlorine that is harmful to wildlife. If you use tap water, fill the pond and then leave it for a week before planting so that the chlorine levels drop. Tap water may encourage duckweed and blanket weed, which can be invasive and reduce oxygen levels in the pond, so keep a look out for these and remove them from the water if you spot them.

LEFT *Grouping pots and plants around a miniature pond makes it more accessible for birds and amphibians, allowing them to get in and out of the water easily.*

## Planting for miniature ponds

Choose a few aquatic plants, considering the depth they require when making your selection. (See Planting a Pond, page 55 for advice on how to plant them or repot as necessary.) Generally, water lilies should be placed in the tub first at a depth of about 10–12in (25–30cm), with marginals going in next, placed on stones if necessary, and then the floating plants on the surface. If possible, surround your pond with potted plants and foliage.

ABOVE *Think about the mature size of the plants when planning your miniature pond, so that they will thrive and not dominate the container.*

# Bog gardens

*A boggy, wet area of a garden can be particularly difficult to deal with, but creating a bog garden can make an attractive feature of it and provide another wildlife-friendly habitat. If you do not have an area that is very wet, you can still think about creating the conditions artificially, and enjoy being able to introduce plants to your garden that would otherwise not be suitable.*

## Suitable bog garden plants

**Giant** or **Chilean Rhubarb**
(*Gunnera manicata*)
(NB: this can grow up to 8ft
[2.5m] tall)

**Turkish** or **Chinese Rhubarb**
(*Rheum palmatum*)
(It looks similar to *Gunnera*, but is much smaller)

**Japanese Water Iris**
(*Iris ensata* var.)

**Water Forget-me-not**
(*Myosotis scorpioides*)

**Mealy Primrose**
(*Primula pulverulenta*)

**Hosta** (*Hosta* species)

## Making a bog garden

**1** To make a bog garden, first decide on the site. Choose an open area that retains water well or is naturally quite wet (though this is not essential). Bog gardens can survive well in sunny spots, but may be harder to keep moist.

**2** Dig out the area to a depth of between 12 and 15in (30 and 40cm), keeping the soil to one side to use later.

**3** Cut some plastic sheeting or a butyl liner large enough to sit inside the hole and lay it in the hole, piercing it a few times with a garden fork to add some drainage holes.

**4** Pour gravel or coarse sand into the bottom to cover the holes so that they do not become blocked with soil.

**5** Tip the soil back into the hole, adding handfuls of well-rotted compost, manure, or leaf mold as you go. Bog garden plants require a nutrient-rich soil, so it is important to add plenty of composted matter.

**6** Leave the soil to settle for a few days and then plant with your chosen plants, having soaked them thoroughly first. Cover the surface of the soil with bark chippings to help retain moisture.

**7** Lay log pieces or stones around the bog garden to cover any plastic that is showing through and create cover for insects. Water the bog garden thoroughly.

**8** Keep the soil moist, watering well in hot, dry weather, especially if the bog garden is in a very sunny spot.

# Creating a bog garden in a container

Alternatively, if you cannot spare enough ground to create a bog garden, then a container bog garden may be the answer. An old wheelbarrow makes a great container and has the added benefit of being mobile, so it can be moved to a warmer spot in winter to protect more delicate plants.

**1** Soak the plants in their pots thoroughly to make sure that the roots are wet before planting.

**2** Add garden soil (or buy topsoil from a garden center if you do not have any in your garden) to the wheelbarrow until it is about two-thirds full.

**3** Take the plants out of their pots, dig holes in the soil, and plant them firmly, leaving the root ball slightly higher than the surface of the soil.

**4** Continue to plant all the plants in the wheelbarrow, adding more soil and firming the soil around them.

**5** Cover the surface with pebbles and stones, which will help to retain moisture and adds a decorative touch.

**6** Water the plants well, and remember to keep the soil moist throughout the year.

RIGHT *This bog garden in a wheelbarrow is suitable for small backyards and terraces, regardless of whether you have any ground to plant in or not. Creating the ideal conditions for bog plants is simple, and the size of the wheelbarrow means that it will be easy to maintain.*

# Birdbaths

*Birdbaths are another important addition to the garden, providing water for birds that need access to it to keep them hydrated throughout the year, and also giving them an opportunity for washing and preening.*

## Choosing a birdbath

Stone pedestal birdbaths look beautiful in a garden, nestled between shrubs and flowers in a border, tempting birds to dip in for a bathe. If you decide to buy a birdbath, remember that birds may not be attracted by bright colors and fancy designs, so bear in mind the practicalities rather than the look. Make sure that the birdbath is not too deep, and avoid glazed surfaces that may be too slippery. Alternatively, you can make one yourself quite easily (see opposite).

## Maintaining a birdbath

1 Keeping the birdbath clean is very important, so add fresh water to it every couple of days, and scrub it with a stiff brush every few weeks to keep it hygienic and disease-free, and to prevent algae from building up.

2 Check the water regularly during the winter to make sure that it has not frozen over, breaking the ice if it has.

3 Place the birdbath in a border with prickly plants around the base to deter cats and keep it away from fences and walls to allow birds to detect predators from afar and give them time to fly away. Although cleaning is important,

LEFT *A traditional stone birdbath fits well into a garden and provides birds with a much-needed supply of water.*

## MAKING A BIRDBATH

1 Find a shallow dish or bowl and attach it to the top of an upturned plant pot using a glue gun.

2 If the inside of the dish is very smooth, put some clean gravel or sand in the bottom to create a rough, non-slip surface. Place a few pebbles in the dish so that birds can drink from the water without getting too wet.

3 Position the birdbath in a shady spot so that the water will not evaporate too much in hot weather, and top it up regularly.

don't use chemicals and detergents in the birdbath because they could harm the birds and other visiting wildlife.

4 Place the birdbath in a fairly low position because birds tend to prefer this. However, if there are lots of cats in your area, it may be safer to raise it a little higher. Birds enjoy bathing, but need to feel safe when doing so.

You may well discover that a whole host of insects find their way to your birdbath, as well as our feathered friends. Wasps and other pollinators will be attracted to the water to drink and cool off during hot weather, so adding a birdbath to your garden brings even more benefits.

# CHAPTER FIVE

# Shelter *and* food *for* wildlife

Places to shelter and a plentiful supply of food for wildlife are surefire ways of encouraging birds, small mammals, amphibians, and insects into your garden, and will benefit you just as much as them as you observe the comings and goings of many different creatures.

Providing birdhouses, bug hotels, and nesting sites for a range of birds, mammals, and insects is easy to do and attracts wildlife by creating environments in which they can nest and shelter throughout the year. Installing feeders and putting out regular supplies of food encourages all kinds of animals into your garden. In particular, it will help wildlife if they have access to the right kind of food during periods when it may not be available naturally in the local area. Whether you make your own shelters and feeders or use store-bought ones, of which there are many on the market, it is really important to include some of them in your garden or balcony.

# Shelter

*Providing shelter and nesting sites for wildlife is relatively easy to do, and they make valuable features in the garden. If you have room, put up a bird box or two on your plot, or make a bug hotel, or hang bee boxes up—just one of these will bring lots of benefits.*

ABOVE *This charming bird box will provide shelter and nesting opportunities for visiting birds. If birds are not tempted into it, then try moving the box to another part of the garden that might be more appealing to them.*

OPPOSITE *Food and nesting sites for birds are important, but helping them out by providing nesting material is a good idea, too. This wooden hanger is packed full of useful materials that birds can use to build their nests.*

## Bird boxes

Whether you make or buy a box, consider where to put it. Avoid placing it near other bird boxes or feeders so that nesting birds will not be disturbed, and choose a spot out of direct sunlight and sheltered from the wind. Make sure it is out of the reach of cats.

Bird houses are often made with a range of sizes of holes or open fronts to suit particular species. Generally, houses with small holes need to be sited 3–10ft (1–3m) from the ground as birds such as blue tits will prefer this. Open bird houses can be placed lower, suiting robins and wrens, but houses with larger holes suitable for sparrows and starlings can be sited in higher positions. When buying a bird house, check to see which birds will be attracted to it, and then place it at the required height, ideally on a tree trunk, but a wall, fence, or shed will do.

## Nesting material

Help our feathered friends out by providing nesting material in a hanger, so that it is easily accessible to many birds. A range of different materials will help several species of birds, because they are often quite choosy about what they use for nest building.

Look for bird feeders that are made from wire mesh so birds will be able to pull the contents out easily. Fill the hanger with a range of things, such as wool from old sweaters, twigs, moss, dried grass, natural twine, and even dog hair. Hang it in the garden from late spring onward, topping it up whenever necessary.

If a mesh hanger is not available, place materials in an empty hanging basket, or leave small mounds of freshly cut grass (starlings particularly like this). Also, create small muddy areas, especially in warm weather, as some species use mud to construct nests.

# Green roofs

The key to wildlife gardening is to use as much outside space as you can to try to increase the number of visiting creatures. Adding a green roof to a birdhouse provides a cozy nesting site for birds and will appeal to bees, butterflies, and moths, too. A store-bought birdhouse is simply adapted by adding wooden battens to the roof, and then planted with low-growing sedum and saxifrage to make an attractive and practical addition to the garden (see page 15 for more information). If you decide to paint your bird box, make sure that the paint is water-based and is safe for birds.

OPPOSITE *A selection of low-growing plants that are drought-tolerant and hardy have been used to create this pretty little green roof on a bird house.*

Plants to try:
*Saxifraga* 'Cloth of Gold'
*Sedum acre* 'Golden Queen', *S. oregonense*, *S. pluricaule*, *S. spathulifolium* 'Purpureum', *S. spurium* 'Fuldaglut'

## TO MAKE A GREEN ROOF

### YOU WILL NEED

**4 battens of 1½ x ¾in (35 x 20mm) wood, cut to the same width as the roof of your bird box**

**2 battens of 1½ x ¾in (35 x 20mm) wood, cut to the same depth (I.e. measuring from back to front) as the roof of your bird box less 1½in (40mm) (the width of 2 battens)**

**Screws and a drill**

**A piece of plastic sheeting cut to the same area as the roof of the bird box with 2–3in (5–7cm) extra on all sides**

**Potting compost**

1 Drill holes in the first four wooden battens about 1in (2.5cm) from each end, place them along the front and back edges of the bird box roof and screw them onto the roof.

2 Drill holes in the second two pieces of timber about 1in (2.5cm) from each end. Place them along the sides of the roof and screw them in place between the front and back edges. Paint the birdhouse and leave it to dry completely.

3 Line the roof with the piece of plastic and staple it inside the edges of the roof with a staple gun. Fold the plastic at the corners so that it fits neatly.

4 Press some potting compost onto the lining. Take the plants out of their pots and break them up into smaller pieces. Spread out the roots to flatten them slightly, then push the plants into the potting compost, pressing down firmly. Continue planting until the roof is covered.

# Bug hotels

Bug hotels are a great way of housing a wide range of insects —from leaf-cutter and mason bees to centipedes, ladybugs, earwigs, beetle larvae, and many others. They are a useful wildlife feature if you are short of space, or like to keep a tidy garden, and if made from natural materials, they can look attractive enough to become a lovely garden feature.

## MAKING A BUG HOTEL

Site your bug hotel in a sheltered spot in the garden and flatten the ground if necessary so that it will have a solid base. You can adjust the quantities of bricks and/or wood to suit the space you have available.

### YOU WILL NEED

**Approximately 24 bricks (collect old ones from local skips, dumpsters, or wastegrounds, but always ask permission before taking anything)**

**3 equal lengths of wooden planking**

**Some curved or flat roof tiles**

**A selection of small logs, pinecones, twigs, dead flower stalks, small pieces of bamboo, leaves, etc**

1 Make two rows of bricks (each row two bricks high), with the space between them matching the length of the wooden planking.

2 Place a roof tile on the ground between the bricks and lay a plank of wood over the top, resting the ends on the bricks.

3 Continue to build up layers of bricks and wooden planks until the basic structure is complete. Don't be tempted to build it too tall as it could become unstable and topple over.

4 Add roof tiles to the top to form a roof to prevent the stack becoming too wet. If you are using flat roof tiles, prop up one end of them to help rainwater run off.

5 Drill holes in the logs to attract bees and put them in between the layers. Push all the bits and bobs that you have collected into the gaps of the stack, cramming them in as necessary. Cardboard, straw, and bits of tree bark are useful, too, because they will rot down and create damp, dark corners.

# Food *for* wildlife

*It is very therapeutic to sit for a while and simply watch birds gathering at a bird table, or fox cubs frolicking on the lawn, and taking the time to enjoy and involve yourself in it is a real treat.*

ABOVE *For a very simple bird feeder, simply push apples onto metal skewers, securing them in place with a cork on the end, and use the handle to hang them on tree branches. Check the feeders regularly, replacing the fruit as necessary.*

A garden rich in flowers, fruit, and seeds with a variety of shrubs, bushes, and trees will provide plenty for wildlife to feast on already, but offering additional food will supplement their diets and ensure that they have some kind of sustenance all year round, especially in the harsh winter months.

Different foods will entice a wide range of visitors and increase the diversity of wildlife in your garden considerably.

## Birds

Feeding birds is particularly important, especially over the winter, but they will benefit all year round because having access to plenty of food in the spring and summer will enable them to use their energy to feed their young. Supplying high-fat food over winter is very important, as they need lots of energy to help them keep warm.

There are many different ways of feeding birds, and employing just one or two methods will benefit them hugely. You can simply throw a few handfuls of food onto the ground, which will appeal to blackbirds, thrushes, wrens, and starlings among others, but you might prefer to use a bird feeder or invest in a bird table.

**Bird feeders** Bird feeders are readily available from garden centers and pet stores, and it is worth buying good-quality ones. Feeders are suitable for smaller birds, and some are specifically designed to prevent access by squirrels, which can be a very good idea. However, avoid feeders made from plastic because they can easily be destroyed by squirrels.

Birds are very susceptible to infection and disease, so it is very important to keep feeders and bird tables clean and to avoid using rotten or moldy food. Wash feeders with warm soapy water, and clean the interiors with a bottle brush every six weeks to keep them hygienic.

# PINECONE BIRD FEEDER

**This pinecone bird feeder is simple to make and looks charming hanging in the garden, supplying the birds with food.**

1 Collect pinecones and hang them upside down for a while to let any insects crawl out. Then wash them before you start, leaving them to dry thoroughly.

2 Take some heavy wire (available from DIY stores) that is flexible enough to bend around the cones and wrap the end around the bottom open scales of a pinecone, twisting the end of the wire around one of the scales so that it is securely attached.

3 Continue to wrap the wire round another pinecone, butting it up closely to the first pinecone. Continue in the same way with several more, until you have a strip of about seven pinecones.

4 Leave a length of wire about 8in (20cm) long at one end and form a hanging loop, twisting the ends together firmly.

5 Take a packet of gelatin and dissolve into ¼ cup (2fl oz/60ml) of hot water, stirring well. Mix in about ¾ cup (5oz/150g) of birdseed and spread the mixture over some greaseproof paper to cool slightly.

6 Press the birdseed mixture into the pinecones, pushing it in firmly between and around the scales.

7 Hang the bird feeder on a hook, adding a raffia bow for decoration if you like. When the birds have finished the food, wash the feeder with a garden hose, then add more of the seed-and-gelatin mix to re-use it.

Trees are the ideal place to hang feeders because they provide shelter and the branches allow easy access. If your garden does not have a tree, it may be worth investing in a specially designed stand that can be sited anywhere and will hold several feeders at once. It is a good idea to move feeders every few weeks in order to reduce the risk of old food building up underneath that may harbor disease. This may also help to deter rats which will be attracted by the scraps.

**Bird tables** As an alternative to feeders, a simple bird table, either a store-bought one or a homemade one, will attract lots of birds, but will also be accessible to larger birds and squirrels. Expect to see sparrows, robins, greenfinches, tits, and pigeons visiting feeders and bird tables.

Wipe bird tables regularly, removing old food, and keep them topped up with fresh food or seeds. Avoid using detergents on feeders and bird tables as they may cause harm to birds.

**Food for birds** Try some of the following foods. Different foods will attract different birds, so it's a good idea to keep a note of which birds visit when.

- Bird seed (always buy good-quality seed).
- Fat balls (remove the plastic mesh bags that they are often sold in, as birds' feet and beaks can get tangled in them—put them in a feeder or hang them from a tree branch).
- Sunflower hearts (these are the seeds of sunflowers with the outer husk removed and are easier for birds to eat than the whole seed).
- Niger seeds (goldfinches love these).
- Plain, unsalted peanuts (always buy good-

# MAKE YOUR OWN BIRD TABLE

1 You will need a wooden post at least 4½ft (1.5m) in length and a flat piece of wood with a surface area of about 24 sq in (60 sq cm) that can be either square or rectangular. You can make the post longer, depending on where you are putting the table and how high you would like it to be.

2 Screw the flat piece of wood, using two or three screws, onto one end of the post and push the other end of the post firmly into the ground so that it won't move in high winds. It may be helpful to shave the end of the post that will be going into the ground into a point to help push it in.

3 If your woodwork skills are good, you could also add two short upright posts and a roof, to help keep the bird food dry.

quality nuts, certified for bird food and chop them during the breeding season as whole nuts can choke baby birds).

• Mealworms and wax worms (available to buy in tubs from garden centers and pet shops or online stores).
• Mild grated cheese
• Dried fruits, such as currants, raisins, and sultanas (soak them in water for a few hours to prevent them swelling in the birds' stomachs).
• Apples, pears, and bananas
• Cooked, unsalted white or brown rice
• Uncooked oatmeal

OPPOSITE *Providing food for birds doesn't have to mean buying expensive feeders or making complicated structures. Simply place dishes of bird feed on a twiggy tree or shrub, or thread monkey nuts onto some wire and hang them in the garden. These will provide valuable energy sources.*

ABOVE *If you are painting your bird table or feeder, make sure that the paint you use is water based and non-toxic, so that it will not cause harm to wildlife.*

# PUMPKIN BIRD FEEDER

**Bird feeders do not have to be practical and dull. This lovely bird feeder uses a beautiful pumpkin half as the shell, with a pretty decoration of cloves around the top, and will be a delightful addition to the garden. Choose pumpkins that are not too big as the feeder may become too heavy, and cram with bird seed to tempt birds from far and near.**

1 Cut the pumpkin in half and scoop out the seeds and flesh with a spoon (unless you have a pumpkin shell left over from cooking).

2 Use a bradawl or skewer to make a line of holes around the top of the cut edge and push a clove into each hole. Make a second row in the same way.

3 Cut two pieces of rope to a length of 3ft (1m). Turn the pumpkin cut side down and lay the two pieces of rope in a cross shape over the middle of the base. Push a nail through both pieces of rope and into the pumpkin. Turn the pumpkin cut side up.

4 Soften a packet of lard or suet at room temperature in a mixing bowl. Mix about twice as much bird seed as lard together and scoop it into the pumpkin half.

5 Find a branch to hang your feeder from and tie the ends of the rope together, finishing with a secure knot.

RIGHT *Siting bird tables near dense shrubs and trees will provide food for nesting birds. It is important to keep the table topped up to give a constant supply of food.*

ABOVE *A hedgehog feeding station offers shelter and protection for hedgehogs and ensures that they get a regular supply of food. Put out the food on a daily basis and clean away any scraps.*

## Hedgehogs

Hedgehogs feed on a wide range of things, but predominantly beetles, slugs (making them a gardener's best friend!), worms, caterpillars, earwigs, and millipedes. They will benefit from additional feeding in very dry or cold periods and in fall to prepare them for hibernation.

Put food out in a shallow dish after sunset (when there are fewer flies around) in a sheltered spot or feeding station if you have one, and clear the dish away in the morning. Leave a shallow dish of water out as well to provide drinking water. Do not feed hedgehogs bread and milk as they are lactose intolerant and this can make them very ill.

**Hedgehog feeding station** A plastic storage box or old wooden box (wine boxes work well) no smaller than 12 x 16in (30 x 40cm) is ideal for this feeding station for little prickly friends.

**1** Mark out a hole at one end about 5in (13cm) square, with one side of the hole on the open top of the box, and cut it out using a jigsaw or hacksaw. Sand the edges to remove any rough bits, or stick tape around the edges if they are sharp.
**2** Put a shallow dish of food and one of water down and cover with the box, making sure that the dishes are on the far side of the box, away from the opening to prevent other animals getting to them. Place a couple of bricks on the top of the box to weigh it down.
**3** Check the dishes in the morning to see if a hedgehog has paid a visit. Clean the dishes, throwing any remnants away. Remember to leave food out regularly to provide a constant supply.

### Food for hedgehogs
Try some of the following foods:
- Good-quality cat or dog food
- Cooked ground/minced meat
- Plain, unsalted, chopped peanuts
- Sunflower hearts (see Food for Birds, page 74)
- Dried mealworms (see Food for Birds, page 75)

### Foxy mischief!

I have discovered that foxes are also very fond of shoes. I found out the hard way when my lovely gardening shoes were tossed round the garden, chewed and left decidedly the worse for wear by a local fox! My tip is always to bring shoes and boots in at the end of the day!

# Squirrels

Squirrels naturally feed on seeds, buds, shoots and bulbs as many gardeners know only too well, as well as insects and bugs. They rarely struggle to find food, but it can be worth leaving out food if you would like to encourage them into your garden, particularly during very hot or very cold weather.

A diet rich in peanuts and dried fruits can cause calcium deficiency, particularly in red squirrels, so also leave out some cuttlefish or bone meal to boost squirrels' calcium levels. Provide foods that are similar to what squirrels would find naturally in the wild and put it out every three or four days, leaving gaps of a week or so every now and then to prevent them from becoming too dependent.

## Food for squirrels

Try some of the following foods:
- Plain, unsalted nuts such as hazelnuts, walnuts, and almonds
- Chopped apples
- Chopped carrots
- Spinach
- Celery

# Foxes

As anyone who has regular visits from foxes will know, they are scavengers and will eat just about anything (a well-fitting lid on trashcans is advisable). You should be cautious when thinking about feeding foxes. Doing so regularly may disrupt their natural scavenging instincts and reduce their territory. Your neighbors may also frown upon feeding them, so bear all this in mind.

However, a variety of good foods can help to maintain healthy foxes and reduce their susceptibility to disease, making them much more appealing garden visitors. Very importantly, remember that foxes are wild animals. Do not encourage them into your home or try and feed them by hand.

## Food for foxes

Try some of the following foods:
- Dog food
- Raw or cooked meat
- Plain, unsalted peanuts
- Raisins
- Fruit
- Raw eggs

# Badgers

Badgers are often seen as pests in domestic gardens, mainly because they have a habit of digging up well-tended lawns and flowerbeds in search of grubs and earthworms. But embracing these tendencies can bring benefits to your garden because they also enjoy feasting on small mammals such as rats and some of the less desirable insects.

Feeding badgers can help to reduce the damage they often cause, and there is no denying that getting the chance to badger watch at such close quarters is a real privilege. Scatter food directly on the ground around your garden and don't forget to put out a dish of water as badgers, especially young ones, often suffer from dehydration.

## Food for badgers

Try some of the following foods:
- Canned pet food
- Seedless grapes
- Apples
- Pears
- Plums
- Plain, unsalted peanuts and brazil nuts

# Bees

*Bees are a vital part of a wildlife garden, and as we now know, their numbers have been in dangerous decline for several years. The exact reason for this is unknown, but it is likely that a mixture of farming methods, using harmful insecticides, viral infections, and the reduced availability of wildflowers have wiped out large numbers of bees.*

ABOVE *Lavender is a real bee magnet, and a must in a wildlife-friendly garden.*

OPPOSITE *Bees feast on nectar and pollen, providing a valuable service in the garden.*

## Bumblebees

Bumblebees are usually furry and are generally larger than solitary bees and honeybees. There are about 250 species of bumblebee in the world, but normally only a few species are present in any one area. Some bumblebees can be found nesting in the ground, under woodpiles, or in holes in the ground. Others will nest above ground in trees or in long grass, so making sure that there are suitable areas in the garden gives them every opportunity to nest.

The queen bee will start to look for an ideal spot in spring, favoring quiet, shady sites where the nest will not be disturbed. Access to pollen and nectar is very important to her at this time to give her energy for the task ahead. When the queen bee settles herself, she will produce her first batch of eggs and will surround herself with worker bees that will collect food and look after the young. There may be up to 400 bees in a nest, although this can vary depending on the time of year. The queen produces males and females, which will mate. The males then die, leaving the female queens to hibernate, often in earth, over winter, ready to begin the process all over again the following spring.

### Common bumblebees

**Buff-tailed bumblebee:** Buff-tailed bumblebees are regulars in our gardens and are recognizable by the yellow band near the head and another one across their abdomens. The queens have buff-colored tails. The male and worker bee tails are white with a slight buff-colored tinge. The worker bees will collect pollen and nectar from a wide variety of flowers. Often the first bees to emerge from hibernation in early spring, they usually nest in the

ground, perhaps in old mouse or vole holes. They have short tongues, so are attracted to open flowers from which they can access the nectar and pollen easily.

**Common carder bee**: Common carder bees are easily identified by their distinctive gingery-brown shaggy "fur." They often nest in grass and on the surface of the ground, and are much smaller than other bumblebees. They feed on plants with relatively long flowers because they have long tongues, and they are attracted to honeysuckle and foxgloves, among other plants. They can be spotted from early spring through to late fall.

**Early bumblebee**: Early bumblebees are very small bees that can be recognized by the bright yellow stripes across their thorax and abdomens, and their orange-red tails.

They nest underground using burrows left by small mammals and pollinate soft fruits, feeding on open flowers with their short tongues. They live in small colonies, emerging in spring.

**Red-tailed bumblebee**: Red-tailed bumblebees are very common and are one of the easiest to recognize with their black bodies and distinctive orange-red tails. The male bees have a thin yellow stripe across the thorax and yellow hair on the head. They are particularly attracted to yellow flowers, and their short tongues require them to look for open flowers like dandelions and daisies. They usually nest underground, and in and around the bases of walls. They emerge in early spring and can be seen right though to fall.

## CREATING NESTING SITES FOR BUMBLEBEES

**Bumblebees will usually find their own nesting sites, but you can help them along the way by creating a nest for them.**

1 Dig a shallow hole in the soil large enough for an upturned flowerpot to sit in. Take a piece of rubber or plastic tubing at least 12in (30cm) long and partially bury it, leaving one end sticking out in the hole and the other end sticking out of the soil for bees to be able to enter.

2 Put the upturned plant pot in place, adding a few handfuls of soft pet bedding, moss, or grass inside it. Cover the plant pot's drainage hole with a tile or slate to keep the inside of the pot dry.

ABOVE *Borage (also known as starflower) looks beautiful in the garden and attracts pollinators with its pretty blue flowers.*

**Solitary bees** Solitary bees are often smaller than bumblebees and can sometimes be mistaken for wasps. They do not live in nests as bumblebees do, but lay eggs in hollow flower stems and holes in wood. Solitary bees leave nectar and pollen for the transforming grubs, which when fully grown will leave their nesting site, ready to mate and start another cycle. Solitary bees often use the same sites for several years, so ensuring that nesting sites and bee boxes are left undisturbed can be important.

**Red mason bees** Recognizable by their gingery fur, they nest in hollow plant stems and walls. Male bees are usually smaller than the females and have white tufts of hair on their faces. The females make nests using pollen and mud, using hollow flower stems and holes in walls to site them. They can be seen from early spring onward.

**Leaf-cutter bees** Leaf-cutter bees are small and are often confused with honeybees. They have distinctive orange hairs on the underside of their abdomen. Leaf-cutter bees cut discs out of leaves (hence the name), particularly rose leaves, which they use to build their nests. These bees nest in hollow flower stems, in walls, and often in dead wood. They emerge in late spring and can be seen around until midsummer.

**Tawny mining bees** The female tawny mining bee is gingery-red, while the male bees are smaller and duller in color. They nest

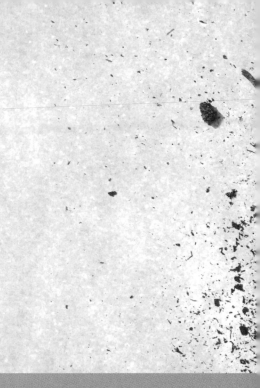

in the ground often in lawns, where they leave small mounds of earth on the surface. They feed on soft fruits, fruit trees, and garden plants, and emerge in late spring and can be seen until early summer.

Honeybees Honeybees are usually to be found in hives set up and maintained by beekeepers. They are less furry than bumblebees and usually smaller. They can vary in color from beige to dark brown and black, and can live in hives with up to 50,000 honeybees. They collect nectar and pollen from a range of different flowers, which they take back to the hive, where it is mixed together to form honey. Unlike bumblebees and solitary bees, honeybees do not hibernate, but simply reduce the numbers in the hive over winter.

## MAKING A BEE BOX

**Including a bee box in your garden will create a home suitable for solitary bees. There are many bee boxes available to buy from garden centers (such as the one shown here), but it is easy to make your own.**

1 Cut a length of drainpipe or heavy-duty cardboard tubing approximately 4in (10cm) long.

2 Cut lengths of bamboo cane measuring about 8in (20cm) long, and push them into the drainpipe or cardboard tube to fill the space tightly.

3 Tie some raffia or string several times round the finished bee box, securing with a knot.

4 Choosing a shady spot, hammer a nail into a fence post at least 3ft (1m) from the ground and hang the bee box from it, tying the raffia onto the nail. Angle the bee box slightly, so that rain will not get into it.

*ABOVE When choosing a location for your hives, it is important to make sure that it is out of the way of passing traffic, so that the bees are not disturbed.*

# Beekeeping

If you would like to start your own beehive and begin what can be an addictive and very rewarding hobby, the best thing to do is contact a local beekeeping organization which will be able to help you, offering first-hand knowledge, tips, and advice. You should also find out about courses, training, and lectures in your area, which are well worth considering. There are many beekeeping books available, too, that can help you with the setting up and running of your hives.

## Location
The location for a hive needs to be considered carefully. Hives need dry, sheltered, and preferably sunny spots, but you don't necessarily need a large garden to have one. Position the hive in a quiet corner of the garden or roof terrace with its entrance pointing away from paths and communal spaces (always bear in mind neighbors and other people who may pass by). Placing hives near high structures, such as walls and hedges (although they need to be 3–4ft/1–1.2m away from these) should help reduce the chances of bees stinging because they will need to fly high over people's heads to get away from the hives.

## Equipment
To start beekeeping, you will need:
- Hive
- Protective clothing (a bee suit and veil to protect the head and face; a good pair of protective gloves that can be cleaned easily; and a stout pair of boots or wellingtons)
- Bee smoker, which will help to subdue the bees if necessary
- Hive tool, which is used to prise the frames and various parts of the hive open and can be used to remove beeswax from inside the hive
- Honey extractor and the equipment to filter the honey

Take advice on choosing all the equipment that you will need, and find a reputable supplier who will be able to kit you out.

Initially, you may choose to start off with a small working colony of about 10,000 bees, increasing the numbers as you become more experienced. Colonies vary a lot with some being much calmer than others, so it is important to source the bees from a reputable supplier who will be able to provide you with a good-tempered colony.

Once up and running, your hive should need no more than half an hour's attention a week, although you may find the comings and goings in the hive so fascinating that you will happily want to devote more time to it.

ABOVE It is worth investing in a hive tool when you start to keep bees, because it has several uses in the hive.

LEFT Wearing protective clothing is essential when caring for bees. Use the correct equipment to ensure that you remain unscathed when opening the hive.

# CHAPTER SIX

# Shrubs, climbers, *and* grasses

Shrubs, climbers, and grasses play an integral part in the garden, adding color, texture, and form. They are all also invaluable to wildlife, and may attract a whole host of visiting birds, insects, amphibians, and small mammals.

In an established garden, you may have several shrubs and climbers already, but it may be possible to feature a few more. Consider the size and health of your shrubs, climbers, and grasses, and add to them accordingly to increase the overall appeal throughout the garden. Before planting, look at the potential size of each plant and consider the ideal conditions to ensure that your shrubs, climbers, and grasses will live long and happy lives.

# Shrubs

*The term "shrub" covers a wide range of plants, from relatively small, bushy, compact ones that keep themselves to themselves to sprawling, fast-growing climbers, which will quickly cover and spread throughout borders and along walls.*

When choosing new shrubs specifically with wildlife in mind, scented flowering shrubs are a good bet. They provide pollen and nectar as well as shelter and shade, followed by berries, which will support birds throughout the colder months. Planting a range of shrubs to offer sustenance and shelter throughout the year will help to make your borders and pots visually more interesting as well, because they will provide color and form all year round. Thorny shrubs, such as hawthorn and berberis, will provide extra protection for nesting birds because their thorns make it harder for predators to attack. Shrubs also shelter a number of insects, such as spiders, caterpillars, and aphids, that will benefit birds like the willow warbler.

The range of shrubs is so large and various that choosing a few for your garden may seem daunting.

However, the list on pages 90–93 gives a few suggestions which all have many wildlife-friendly qualities and look beautiful, too.

## Where to plant shrubs

Before planting shrubs, think about what they will offer your garden and how they will sit with existing plants and features. They will hopefully be in the garden for some considerable time and so require a little more planning and thought than annuals and wildflowers. Consider the following:

● The conditions required for each plant: check with the garden center or nursery when you buy them to make sure that they will be suitable for your garden, so that they will thrive and bloom.

● If you have the space to grow several plants, look at shrubs that provide interest at different times of the year to give wildlife as much choice as possible by way of shelter and food. Choose plants that will furnish the garden with a range of flowers, foliage, berries, and nuts throughout the year. Birds tend to be attracted to red and black berries, so growing plenty of these on several shrubs will supply them with a lot of food.

ABOVE LEFT *Leaving climbers and shrubs to scramble through each other will provide shelter for many insects and birds.*

OPPOSITE *Growing a range of plants in the garden will appeal to a whole host of wildlife and they will look beautiful, too.*

## When to plant shrubs

Plant shrubs between late fall and early spring, avoiding very wet or cold weather, which may prevent adequate root growth. Placing several different shrubs together can increase the benefits to wildlife because they will be able to move from one shrub to another easily, protected from predators. Consider also the size that each shrub may grow to and bear that in mind when planting to avoid overcrowding.

## Planting shrubs

Shrubs are usually sold in containers, but are also available as bare-rooted plants. Do check them to ensure that they have a healthy root system before you buy them. Carefully remove the pot and check that the plant is not too root-bound, or infested with bugs.

**1** Dig a hole at least twice the size of the shrub's pot or root ball, and mix some compost or well-rotted manure into the soil that has been removed. Preparing the soil well before planting is a must so that the shrubs get off to the best possible start.
**2** Take the shrub out of its pot (if it has one) and place it in the hole. The surface of the soil around the shrub in the pot should be level with the surface of the surrounding soil, so add or take away soil from the bottom of the hole as necessary.
**3** Backfill the hole around the shrub with the soil and compost or manure mix, and firm the soil down. Carefully tread round the plant with your heel and water well.
**4** Adding a mulch of compost or bark around the shrub will help to conserve moisture as the roots should not be allowed to dry out until the plant is established. Shrubs will benefit from being fed in spring, using organic fertilizers at the start of the growing season.

BELOW *Before planting shrubs, it is important to prepare the soil to give them the best start and to ensure that the shrubs are healthy and vigorous.*

# Choosing shrubs

The following shrubs will look great in any garden and benefit wildlife:

**Barberry** (*Berberis thunbergii*): an evergreen shrub with bright orange flowers appearing from mid-spring followed by blue berries and spiny stems. Tolerates most soils, but prefers moist, well-drained soil in full sun or partial shade. Requires little pruning. Provides ground cover and berries for birds such as thrushes. Attracts bees and butterfly and moth caterpillars. Thorns protect nesting birds from predators.
Max height: 10ft (3m). Max spread: 10ft (3m)

**Butterfly bush** (*Buddleja davidii*): a fast-growing deciduous shrub whose lilac or white flowers bloom from summer to fall. Prefers fertile, well-drained soil in full sun. Hard pruning in spring will keep it compact. Not called the butterfly bush for nothing, it attracts huge numbers of butterflies, as well as bees and moths.
Max height: 10ft (3m). Max spread: 15ft (4.6m)

**Californian lilac** (*Ceanothus* species): an evergreen shrub that produces masses of vivid blue, white, or pink flowers in spring and early summer. Likes a sheltered spot in full sun. Does not require much pruning, but can be cut back a little after flowering to reduce its size. Do not cut into old wood because it may not re-grow. It attracts hawkmoths, bees, and hoverflies and may attract robins, sparrows, and dunnocks.
Max height: 20ft (6m). Max spread: 26ft (8m)

**Common elder** (*Sambucus nigra*): a shrub that produces white flowers in early summer followed by black glossy berries, and which has attractive green leaves that turn dark purple, then red in winter. Prefers fertile, well-drained soil in sun or part shade. It will produce healthy foliage if cut down to ground level each spring and mulched with plenty of organic

ABOVE *Buddleja is often found on waste ground, but can be a pretty and very wildlife-friendly addition to the garden, guaranteed to appeal to butterflies.*

matter. It attracts moth caterpillars, which feed on the foliage, bees, and wasps, which are attracted by the scent. Thrushes, chaffinches, bullfinches, and blackbirds will eat the berries, while dormice and other small mammals feed on the flowers and berries.
Max height: 20ft (6m). Max spread: 20ft (6m)

**Cotoneaster** (*Cotoneaster lacteus*): an evergreen shrub that produces white or pale pink flowers from spring onward, followed by red berries. Prefers moderately fertile, well-drained soil, but is really not very choosy and will grow in most soils, in sun or partial shade. It requires little pruning, but can be cut down to size if it outgrows its space, without suffering any ill effects. Its flowers attract bees, butterflies, and other insects. Moth caterpillars feed on its foliage, and waxwings, fieldfare, and blackcaps are attracted to the berries and insects that congregate on it.
Max height: 13ft (4m). Max spread: 13ft (4m)

ABOVE *Holly can be trained into a neat tree shape as well as grown along a fence or wall.*

Daphne (*Daphne mezereum*): deciduous shrub that produces scented, pink flowers in late winter followed by red berries. Prefers well-drained, moisture-retentive soil, but does not like to be waterlogged. Likes a shady site. Daphnes do not need pruning. All parts of the plant are poisonous to humans, and the plant gives out a sap that can be a skin irritant, so it is better to avoid this plant if you have children using your garden. It attracts bees, butterflies, and birds among other wildlife.
Max height: 4ft (1.2m). Max spread: 3ft (1m)

Firethorn (*Pyracantha*): an evergreen shrub that produces white flowers in spring followed by red or orange berries in fall to winter if in full sun or part shade, although it may produce fewer berries if it's in too much shade. Grow it in well-drained fertile soil. It flowers on the previous year's growth, so prune it in spring when it is in flower to prevent too many flowering branches being pruned off. It provides shelter and berries for waxwings and song thrushes among other birds, and bees, butterflies, and hoverflies love the flowers.
Max height: 10ft (3m). Max spread: 10ft (3m)

Guelder rose (*Viburnum opulus*): a vigorous, deciduous shrub with just about all-year-round interest that produces beautiful white, lace-cap-like flowers in late spring followed by red berries and red foliage in fall. Prefers well-drained, moist soil in sun or partial shade. It attracts marmalade hoverfly, redwings, bullfinches, and mistle thrushes.
Max height: 15ft (4.6m). Max spread: 13ft (4m)

Holly (*Ilex aquifolium*): an evergreen, spiny-leaved shrub that produces small, white flowers followed by red berries. Male and female flowers grow on separate plants, so both male and female plants must be planted together to get berries. Prefers a moist, well-drained soil and is not particularly fussy about soil types. Prefers sunny sites, but will tolerate partial shade. It attracts bees and holly blue butterfly caterpillars. Holly has berries for a long period so it is popular with many birds, including blackbirds,

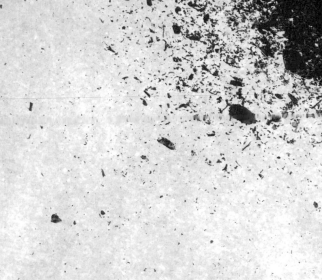

redwings, and thrushes. Dense cover encourages robins and dunnocks to nest, with small mammals hibernating around the base.
Max height: Above 49ft (12m). Max spread: 26ft (8m)

**Hydrangea** (*Hydrangea paniculata*): a fast-growing deciduous shrub that produces large, showy, conical, white flower heads (it is worth it for the flowers alone, which are one of my favorites) from summer through to early fall. Prefers part shade in a fertile and moisture-retentive soil, because it does not like to dry out. Mulch in early spring with organic matter, and prune at the same time, cutting back the previous year's shoots by about a third. Bees find it very attractive. Avoid other hydrangeas that may have sterile flowers—they will have been cultivated so that they flower for a long period, but will not set seed and are of little value to wildlife.
Max height: 10ft (3m). Max spread: 8ft (2.5m)

**Spindle tree** (*Euonymus fortunei*): a compact shrub with green leaves and white edges, that produces small, unspectacular greenish-white, nectar-rich flowers followed by colorful fruit. Prefers moist, well-drained soil in sun or partial shade, but leaf color is better in full sun. Prune in spring, cutting back by a third. It attracts bees, butterflies (including the holly blue butterfly), hoverflies, and moths. Provides shelter for ladybugs, starlings, and sparrows, as well as aphids, and berries for food.
Max height: 3ft (1m). Max spread: Beyond 4ft (1.2m)

BELOW Pyracantha *will provide food for birds throughout the winter as well as shelter in its dense growth.*

# Climbers

*Use walls and fences, and grow climbers that provide vital shelter and food for birds and insects and make a feature of an otherwise dull area. By using a vertical space, climbers offer a great opportunity to grow a relatively large plant in a small area and create dense cover and nesting sites as well as food on a small balcony or in a courtyard garden.*

ABOVE *Plant jasmine near your house so that you can enjoy its wondrous scent and watch the many insects and birds that will be attracted to it.*

Climbers can also provide a link between outside spaces, making it easier for wildlife to move from garden to garden, sheltered from predators.

There are many climbers that are beneficial to wildlife: some for shelter and nesting, others for flowers rich in nectar and pollen, and some providing berries and seeds through the winter. Several provide all these—see pages 96–97. Dense growth encourages robins, wrens, and sparrows to nest and gives shelter to spiders, butterflies, and hoverflies.

Flowering climbers will attract bees, butterflies, hoverflies, and moths, and the berries and seeds that appear later in the season will feed many birds, such as thrushes, warblers, and bullfinches, if you are lucky.

## Support for climbers

Trellis, or wire supports held in place with vine eyes, increases the spread of a plant and help to secure it in place. Put whichever type of support you choose in place before you plant the climbers against the chosen wall or fence. Ideally, leave a gap of about 4in (10cm) between the wall or fence and the supports (add wooden battens to the wall and fix the supports to those) to provide more space for nesting and shelter. It's very important to make sure that the supports are securely attached because plants can become heavy as they establish themselves. Alternatively, plant climbers against pergolas or arches, and again make sure that the structure is secure and strong enough to support the plant.

# Planting climbers

When planting climbers, always position them at least 12in (30cm) away from the neighboring wall or fence, as these can be very dry areas.

**1** Soak the plant in water for at least half an hour before planting.

**2** Dig a hole larger than the pot, adding compost or well-rotted manure to the base of the hole and a handful of blood, fish, and bone meal or seaweed feed to the hole.

**3** Remove the plant from the pot and put it into the hole. (Clematis should always be planted 2–4in/5–10cm below the surface of the surrounding soil to encourage growth from the stem. Other climbers can be planted with their soil's surface level with that of the surrounding ground.)

**4** Backfill the hole around the plant and firm the soil. Water well.

**5** Untie and untwine the stems of the climber gently and fan the stems out, tying them onto your supports or trellis with garden twine, being careful not to damage them.

**6** Tie new growth in regularly and prune any straggly stems to encourage thick, bushy growth.

When the climber is well established, it should provide dense cover for birds. To increase the opportunities for nesting, consider fixing a nesting box within the climber, which will also help to protect birds from predators.

ABOVE *Use vertical structures to increase the growing opportunities in your garden. Wooden obelisks and arches can create good, and relatively secure, nesting sites when covered in climbers, and they will look beautiful, too.*

## Climbers for wildlife

Try some of the following climbers to attract wildlife into your garden or yard:

**Dog rose** (*Rosa canina*): a scrambling climber that produces pretty pink or white fragrant flowers from early summer, followed by red rosehips. Likes moist, well-drained soil in full sun. Cut back a few of the older stems in spring, leaving the rest to scramble up the support. It attract aphids, which provide food for birds. It also provides shelter for sparrows among other birds, who feed on the rosehips.
Max height: 13ft (4m). Max spread: 8ft (2.5m)

**Honeysuckle** (*Lonicera periclymenum*): a deciduous, woody climber that produces fragrant white, yellow, and pink flowers throughout the summer followed by red berries after hot summers.

Prefers moist, well-drained, fertile soil with shade at the base. Cut back by a third after flowering. Apply a thick mulch of organic matter in early spring. It attracts bumblebees, butterflies, and moths. It also provides shelter and berries for thrushes and warblers among other birds.
Max height: 26ft (8m). Max spread: 5ft (1.5m)

**Ivy** (*Hedera helix*): one of the best climbers for wildlife, this self-clinging, evergreen climber with woody stems produces dark green leaves and black berries throughout winter. It can be kept in check with pruning. Tolerates full sun, partial shade, or full shade, and is happy in well-drained soil, but is not particularly fussy. It attracts wasps, hoverflies, bees, and butterflies. Holly blue caterpillars feed on its flower buds and it provides cover and berries for thrushes and blackbirds. Ivy has a reputation for causing damage to bricks and walls, but rather than it being the cause of the damage, it is generally the case that it exacerbates an existing weakness, so before planting, check that the bricks or stones and mortar of the wall you are planting against are in a good enough condition to support this heavy, dense plant.
Max height: 30ft (10m). Max spread: Varies.

**Jasmine** (*Jasminum officinale*): a deciduous climber that produces masses of fragrant (particularly in the evening) white flowers. Likes well-drained, moist soil in sun or partial shade, in a sheltered spot. The flowers will be more fragrant in sunny sites. Prune out old shoots after flowering. It attracts insects, especially moths drawn to the fragrant, white flowers.
Max height: 26ft (8m). Max spread: 8ft (2.5m)

**Old man's beard** (*Clematis vitalba*): a deciduous climber that produces green flowers in summer followed by fluffy seed heads. Likes moist, well-

drained soil in sun or partial shade, but as with most clematis, it likes its feet to be in shade. Cut it back in spring, but this fast grower will put on several feet/meters of growth in one year. It attracts bees, butterflies, hoverflies, and moth caterpillars, and provides shelter and seeds for birds. There are so many clematis, many much smaller, which suit a more compact urban wildlife garden. Choose varieties with open flowers, avoiding the hybrids that will be less beneficial to wildlife.
Max height: 30ft (10m). Max spread: 8ft (2.5m)

## Potato vine (*Solanum jasminoides*): a vigorous
evergreen climber that is covered in masses of pretty little white flowers from spring to early fall. It is a great plant for covering a plain area quickly. Likes fertile, moist, well-drained soil in sun or partial shade. Prune back about a third of the older stems to the ground in spring. It attracts bumblebees, ladybugs, and lacewings.
Max height: 26ft (8m). Max spread: 10ft (3m)

## Wisteria (*Wisteria floribunda*): a vigorous
flowering climber that produces beautiful hanging flowers in lilac and white, from early summer. Prefers moist, well-drained soil in sun or partial shade. Wisteria needs pruning in late winter or early spring to prepare it for flowering, and again in summer to tidy it up. The flowers attract pollinating insects and the thick foliage may encourage blackbirds and robins to nest.
Max height: 26ft (8m). Max spread: 5ft (1.5m)

OPPOSITE *Honeysuckle flowers can smell beautiful and attract lots of insects. The berries that follow will feed birds as well as look wonderful in the garden.*

BELOW *Ivy brings benefits to the garden all year round, but the attractive pompom flowers are particularly appealing to butterflies and wasps.*

# Grasses

*Ornamental grasses bring delicate beauty to the garden, adding form, texture, and shape to a flower border throughout the year. Dotting them around the garden will soften the look of your borders and benefit wildlife hugely.*

ABOVE *Golden oats (Stipa gigantea) is a fairly robust grass that grows well in most conditions.*

From the golden shimmer of *Stipa gigantea* to the billowing clouds of *Deschampsia cespitosa*, grasses also provide shelter and food for a whole host of wildlife: food for many butterflies and moths, seeds for birds, and shelter for spiders and many other insects. They are a must-have in the wildlife garden.

## Where to plant grasses

Dot them around the garden, throughout borders, or grow them in pots or around the edge of the lawn to help wildlife and provide a spot of wild beauty. One of the good things about grasses is that they require little maintenance and are perfect for dry gardens that are prone to drought. Leave them over winter, and cut them back in spring ready for a burst of new growth.

## Grasses for wildlife

I am a relatively new fan of grasses, having considered them rather old fashioned and a little dull for many years, but I am now an absolute convert and have fallen for their charms, and realizing their wildlife-attracting qualities, I now consider them a must.

Try some of the following, which are all very good at attracting wildlife and look particularly beautiful, too:

**Bowles's golden grass** (*Milium effusum* 'Aureum'): a semi-evergreen perennial grass with arches of yellowy green foliage that produce yellow flowers from early summer. Prefers moist soil in sun or partial shade. It seeds freely, which attracts birds who feed on the seeds, and provides cover for insects.
Max height: 2ft (60cm). Max spread: 2ft (60cm)

**Golden oats** (*Stipa gigantea*): an evergreen, perennial grass that produces fluffy-looking, purplish-green, oat-shaped flowers in spring and early summer, which fade to a beautiful golden colour. It looks good all year round. Prefers moderately fertile, well-drained soil in full sun. Cut it back in spring. Its seeds attract finches among other birds, and it provides shelter for insects.
Max height: 8ft (2.5m). Max spread: 3ft (1m)

**Quaking grass** (*Briza media*): a perennial grass that produces greeny-purple, heart-shaped flowers from early to late spring that fade to a straw color over winter. Prefers moist, well-drained, fertile soil in full sun or light shade. Its seeds are eaten by sparrows, finches, and yellowhammers.
Max height: 36in (90cm). Max spread: 12in (30cm)

**Tufted hair grass** (*Deschampsia cespitosa*): an evergreen grass with delicate silvery purple spikes that create a soft, cloud-like effect from spring to fall. Prefers well-drained soil and can withstand quite dry conditions in full sun or partial shade. Remove flower heads after flowering to allow new growth. It offers food for butterfly and moth caterpillar, and provides shelter for spiders.
Max height: 5ft (1.5m). Max spread: 3ft (1m)

**Yorkshire fog** (*Holcus lanatus*): a perennial grass that produces soft, grey–green tufts of leaves with tightly packed flower heads from late spring to midsummer. Prefers well-drained, sunny spots. Commonly found in wild grassland, it suits meadow planting well. It attracts small skipper and wall brown butterfly caterpillars.
Max height: 3ft (1m). Max spread: Varies

ABOVE *Quaking grass (Briza media), with its attractive heart-shaped flowers, is fully hardy and is a welcome addition to any border.*

# CHAPTER SEVEN

# Plant havens
# *for* insects *and* birds

Most gardeners strive to create a garden bursting with color and fragrance. Luckily for us, that is exactly what attracts wildlife into the garden, too. Nectar- and pollen-rich flowers—from crocuses and snowdrops in winter to foxgloves, cornflowers, and lavender in summer—will not only look beautiful but also entice wildlife, providing them with energy and shelter.

Bees and butterflies are important garden visitors. They pollinate plants, which helps to provide food among other things for both us humans and other wildlife. With the decline in their numbers in recent years, it is especially important that we create insect-friendly gardens.

# Flowers *and* fragrance

*One of the best ways to encourage bees, butterflies, and moths into the garden is to provide plenty of flowering plants for as much of the year as possible, ideally from late winter until the following fall, giving the insects a constant supply of food.*

Fragranced plants with colorful blooms are particularly useful. They are rich in pollen and nectar, and offer the added benefit of creating a beautiful border as well.

Grouping flowering plants together, rather than dotting them around the garden, encourages bees to move from one plant to another and including a wide variety of plants benefits several different species of bee, butterfly, and moth. Think about a traditional cottage garden and you won't go far wrong. Packed with color, scent, and old-fashioned, native plants, these pretty, flower-packed gardens are magnets for wildlife of all kinds. See pages 104–105 for plant suggestions for all seasons.

ABOVE *Scented flowers are particularly attractive to pollinating insects. Including some in your garden will entice bees, butterflies, and moths to visit.*

# Choosing plants

*Choose older varieties of flowers and avoid double-flower cultivars because often they don't have much nectar and are hard for bees to enter. In particular, lavender and giant scabious are alive with bees in my garden over the summer and I highly recommend both of them, along with hollyhocks, honeysuckle, and salvia.*

Avoid bedding plants (especially F1 hybrids, which have been overbred and contain little or no nectar or pollen) because they are of little interest to bees. Many flowering plants are available to buy from garden centers, or from nurseries via the Internet, and even supermarkets (be wary of plants from the latter—I find that many are not particularly healthy specimens because they are not often watered regularly). Annuals can be grown from seed and this is a much more economical way of gardening.

## Pest control

All plants, including flowering plants, are susceptible to attacks by insects. For example, many dahlias (though not all, so check which ones you choose) are good for wildlife. With their profusions of showy flowers in vivid pinks, burnt oranges, and deep magentas they make a stunning addition to the garden and attract many pollinating insects, but they are particularly susceptible to slugs in their early stages and earwigs when in flower and can be tricky to grow. For more information on how to ward off insect attacks and control slugs etc, see Preventing Pests, pages 22–23).

## Deadheading

Deadheading flowering plants in your garden will help to keep them flowering for longer so looking at each plant regularly and cutting off flowers that have "gone over" will prevent them from going to seed too early and will provide nectar and pollen for as long as possible.

ABOVE *Bees and butterflies love the tufty flowers of the Blazing Star plant* (Liatris spicata), *which will grow well in a sunny spot in a border or a container.*

# Recommended plants to grow

*Below is a list of flowering plants listed in seasons, including bulbs, perennials, and annuals that will fit perfectly into a wildlife garden and can all be grown very easily.*

ABOVE *Nectar- and pollen-rich foxgloves make striking border plants and will attract bees and moths.*

OPPOSITE *The elegant daisy-like flowers of echinacea attract pollinating insects into the garden, especially butterflies.*

## Spring

**Common Bluebell** (*Hyacinthoides non-scripta*)
**Common Lungwort** (*Pulmonaria officinalis*)
**Forget-me-not** (*Myosotis sylvatica*)
**Foxglove** (*Digitalis* species)
**Honesty** (*Lunaria annua*)
**Primrose** (*Primula vulgaris*)
**Rosemary** (*Rosmarinus officinalis*)
**Wood Spurge** (*Euphorbia amygdaloides*)

## Bulbs

**Crocus** (*Crocus* species)
**Daffodil** (*Narcissus* species)
**Ornamental Onion** (*Allium* species)

## Summer

**Argentinian Vervain** (*Verbena bonariensis*)
**Common Lavender** (*Lavandula angustifolia*)
**Cornflower** (*Centaurea cyanus*)
**Foxglove** (*Digitalis* species)
**Giant Scabious** (*Cephalaria gigantia*)
**Globe Thistle** (*Echinops* species)
**Hollyhock** (*Alcea rosea*)
**Ice Plant** (*Sedum spectabile*)
**Macedonian Scabious** (*Knautia macedonica*)
**Meadow Cranesbill** (*Geranium pratense*)
**Oriental Poppy** (*Papaver orientale*)
**Peony** (*Paeonia* species)
**Purple Coneflower** (*Echinacea purpurea*)
**Sage** (*Salvia officinalis*)
**Tobacco Plant** (*Nicotiana sylvestris*)

**Viper's Bugloss** (*Echium vulgare*)
**Yarrow** (*Achillea millefolium*)

## Annuals

**Common or Pot Marigold** (*Calendula officinalis*)
**Honeywort** (*Cerinthe major*)
**Love-in-a-mist** (*Nigella damascena*)
**Nasturtium** (*Tropaeolum majus*)
**Poached Egg Plant** (*Limnanthes douglasii*)
**Sunflower** (*Helianthus annuus*)
**Sweet Pea** (*Lathyrus* species)

# Fall

**Annual or Sweet Scabious** (*Scabiosa atropurpurea*)
**Carmichael's Monkshood** or **Chinese Aconite** (*Aconitum carmichaelii*)
**Chinese or Japanese Anemone** (*Anemone hupehensis*)
**Dahlia** (*Dahlia* species)
**Michaelmas Daisy** (*Aster* species)
**Red Valerian** (*Centranthus rubra*)

# Winter

**Eastern Cyclamen** (*Cyclamen coum*)
**Heather** (*Erica carnea*)
**Winter-flowering Honeysuckle** (*Lonicera fragrantissima*)
**Winter-flowering Jasmine** (*Jasminum nudiflorum*)
**Winter-flowering Pansy** (*Viola* hybrids)
**Winter Hellebore** (*Hellebore* species)

## Bulbs

**Common Snowdrops** (*Galanthus nivalis*)
**Crocus** (*Crocus* species)
**Grape Hyacinth** (*Muscari armeniacum*)

## SEED BOMBS

Make the perfect gift for flower-loving friends with these wildflower seed bombs. Throw them onto bare soil or grassy areas, let nature take its course, and wait for the flowers to bloom. Hopefully they will also drop seeds at the end of summer, and these will then produce more plants and more flowers in subsequent years.

1 Use air-drying modeling clay (available from art stores), which will hold the seed bombs together but break down easily as the seeds grow. Put the clay in a bowl, breaking it up into small pieces.

2 Put a couple of handfuls of potting compost in the bowl with a little water and squish and mix it all together with your hands.

3 Mix about two packets of wildflower seeds into the bowl, making sure that the seeds are evenly distributed.

4 Break off bits of the mixture about the size of a walnut and roll into balls. Put them on a tray and leave to dry for a day or two.

5 Seed bombs are best used in the spring, so that the seeds will have the right conditions to grow. To use them, simply throw them onto open ground, wait for rain (it will help the clay to disintegrate), and keep an eye out for a range of wildflowers that will hopefully bloom a few weeks later.

## Sunflower-head feeders

Sunflower seeds are a great year-round bird food, with a high fat content that provides valuable energy. They are also great fun to grow from seed, especially for children who take great delight in competing to see whose plant can grow the tallest.

Cut sunflower heads down after flowering and hang them upside down from a branch or fence, tying a few strands of raffia or twine around the stems to secure them in place.

ABOVE AND RIGHT *Sunflowers provide a rich source of pollen and nectar when in full bloom, and the seeds are a great source of food for birds.*

# CHAPTER EIGHT

# Growing fruit *and* vegetables

Growing your own fruit and vegetables has to
be one of the most addictive and rewarding aspects of
gardening. From the pleasure of digging and preparing
the soil, the joy of sitting down with a pile of seed
catalogs and deciding which fruit and vegetable crops
to grow, to the ultimate delight of unearthing your first
crop of potatoes and gathering your first basket
of beans, growing your own food is something that
every gardener should try.

Whether you have the room to devote a large area
of your garden to food production, or raised beds, or
the space for just a few pots and window boxes,
I encourage you to have a go.

# Wildlife: friends *and* enemies

*While fruit and vegetables may not be what first springs to mind when thinking about wildlife gardening, it is worth noting that many crops rely on insects to pollinate them, so a wildlife-friendly garden that encourages a range of insects, birds, and mammals onto your plot can only benefit the fruit and vegetable patch.*

Much fruit and vegetable gardening is about pest control and protecting crops from the insects and bugs that wildlife-friendly gardening tries to encourage, so the two may seem at odds with each other.

However, a rich diversity of insects, birds, and invertebrates will also help to provide natural pest control, letting your crops flourish and your fruit bushes thrive.

Taking a more generous approach and welcoming the many benefits that wildlife can bring, being prepared to share your crops a little more and working in partnership with your tiny garden visitors will promote a healthier and happier garden for all.

Encouraging bees to pollinate your fruit bushes, letting birds feast on the fruits by leaving some of them un-netted, and accepting that you will lose a few strawberries to slugs and woodlice, will allow you to appreciate the benefits that these "pests" in the garden bring, to reap bountiful harvests, and live happily with them.

---

Be vigilant! One of the best ways of growing healthy crops is to inspect them regularly and address any problems quickly before they get the chance to take hold. Physical intervention is an effective way of removing caterpillars, aphids, and slugs and snails, feeding your finds to birds or hedgehogs. A quick blast with the hosepipe should get rid of aphids if there is a particularly bad infestation, and better still, encouraging ladybugs onto the plant will help both you and them.

# Protecting crops

*There are many ways of protecting fruit and vegetable crops from hungry wildlife without having to use garden chemicals. As well as the suggestion mentioned here, companion planting —using combinations of plants to encourage or deter pests— can be a very effective method (see pages 118–125).*

Creating barriers around fruit and vegetables helps to prevent damage from wildlife: netting fruit bushes to protect berries from birds, covering carrot seedlings with horticultural fleece to shield them from carrot root fly, and covering cabbages with fleece to prevent caterpillar damage will give your plants a head start, but leave some of your plants and seedlings uncovered so that insects, birds, and mammals will have access to food.

Leaving a few fruit bushes uncovered for the birds, or a cabbage or two for cabbage white butterflies, will offer valuable benefits not just to the wildlife but to you as well. If you do decide to net your crops, then make sure that alternative food sources are available in other areas of your garden.

## Cages, fleece, and netting

There are many different types of fruit and vegetable cage available in garden centers or from online retailers, but you can simply cover your plants with horticultural fleece or old net curtains or netting, stretching them over garden canes if necessary. It's a much cheaper and very effective alternative.

**1** Anchor the netting or fleece with stones round the edges to keep them in place.
**2** Make sure that there are no gaps in the netting, as birds may get in and become stuck inside.
**3** Bear in mind that while covering your crops will help to prevent predators from damaging them, it will also prevent some beneficial bugs from getting to the plants.

OPPOSITE *Growing healthy crops is the first step toward preventing pest damage. Keep your plot fed and watered to produce strong, robust plants that will be less susceptible to attack.*

ABOVE *Netting blueberries will protect the fruits, although consider leaving a few un-netted to feed the birds.*

# Creating a healthy plot

*Soil improvement is the first and most important thing that you can do when growing food, and will reap great rewards. Add home-made compost (or store-bought if that is not available) or well-rotted manure to the ground before planting out seeds and seedlings to give them the best start, provide them with nutrients, and aid moisture retention.*

## Soil improvement

If your garden has very heavy soil, try adding leaf mold and mushroom compost (again, available from garden centers) to break it up and prepare the soil for vegetable crops.

Each crop will require different conditions for growth, from lettuce, which will happily grow in fairly nutrient-poor soil, to tomatoes, which love rich, freshly composted soil and regular feeding. So consider the individual needs of each plant when deciding where to grow them and you will have happier, healthier produce that will be less prone to attack.

LEFT *Digging in compost or well-rotted manure prior to planting will give your crops the best possible start. Whether you make your own compost or buy it from a garden center, preparing the soil will provide your plants with the nutrients they require. Putting in the effort at an early stage really will bring great benefits!*

## Garden organically

Artificial chemicals, such as insecticides and fertilizers, are used in fruit and vegetable plots more than in any other area of the garden as we battle to contain slug damage or endeavor to grow more and more abundant crops, but they can cause serious damage to visiting wildlife.

## Going to seed

Leaving a few of each crop to go to seed not only looks beautiful but will also feed birds and bees, and it's a very easy way to provide food. From the twisted beauty of tall onion and garlic stems to the delicate umbels of fennel and the dainty flowers of carrots left to go to flower (which are particularly attractive to hoverflies and wasps), providing valuable food for many insects as well as ourselves could not be easier.

## Pollinating plants

Grow annuals and flowering plants around and alongside fruit and vegetables to encourage wildlife and increase pollination. This in turn will increase crops and provide you with a bountiful harvest. Bees, moths, and butterflies are all welcome visitors to the fruit and vegetable garden and are attracted by flower borders, wildlife areas, and nettles. So nettle patches and areas of long grass near vegetable beds will be beneficial, too.

ABOVE *The delicate yellow umbels of fennel are particularly attractive to hoverflies.*

# What to grow

*The key to fruit, vegetable, and herb growing is to grow crops that you actually like to eat. This may sound obvious, but in the past I have spent time and given over valuable space in my garden to crops that my family weren't at all interested in eating. So now I concentrate on things that we love, which grow well in our garden, and suit the amount of time that we can devote to them.*

Deciding what to grow to eat is a purely personal matter, but here are a few crops that, as well as being tasty and relatively easy to grow, also have benefits for wildlife. Many fruit and vegetables are pollinated by both wind and insects, but some rely solely on bees. Growing fruit and vegetables in a wildlife-friendly garden encourages insects into your garden and also benefits the crops.

## Vegetables
### Vegetables that rely on insects to pollinate them:
Runner beans
Fava (broad) beans
Pumpkins
Squash
Tomatoes

### Vegetables that attract insects:
Cabbages (attract butterflies)
Carrots (attract hoverflies and wasps)
Leeks (flowers attract bees)
Onions (flowers attract bees)

LEFT *Throw a few nasturtium seeds into a container when growing vegetables such as squash. As well as looking pretty, the flowers will help to reduce aphid attacks.*

# Fruit

Many fruits are perfect for the wildlife garden as berry-producing plants are particularly beneficial to birds.

Redcurrants and white currants are really worth growing. Birds are particularly fond of them and so, in true wildlife-friendly style, why not net some of them and leave some for the birds to feast on.

Raspberries, blackberries, and alpine strawberries are all great for bees, as are blueberries, which blackbirds particularly like.

Fruit trees such as apple, plum, pear, and cherry will all help to feed birds as well as providing shelter and nesting sites.

## Fruits that rely on insects to pollinate them:

Apples
Apricots
Pears
Plums
Strawberries
Sweet cherries

## Fruits that attract insects:

Blackcurrants
Fruit trees, such as apple, plum, and cherry
Quince
Redcurrants

# Herbs

Herbs are very easy to grow, and, once established, can pretty much be left to their own devices. Used for centuries for their culinary and medicinal qualities, many also have very attractive flowers or foliage and fit in well in flower borders and containers. They are also magnets for bees, butterflies, moths, hoverflies, and birds.

If you use herbs regularly in the kitchen, the plants may not get to the stage where they set seed, but if you leave some of them to flower, it will benefit birds, too. Leave dead flower stems and leaves in situ over winter and cut the plants back in early spring so that they provide food and shelter for as long as possible.

Herbs tend to favor sunny, sheltered spots and are happy growing in containers, which stops them becoming too invasive and means that you can dot them around your garden in borders alongside flowering plants.

## Herbs to grow

**Angelica** (*Angelica* species): a tall, striking plant that attracts bees and hoverflies. Birds feed on the seeds

**Bergamot** (*Monarda* species): spiky, red-pink flowers that attract bees

**Borage** (*Borago officinalis*): pretty blue flowers that attract bees, butterflies, and hoverflies

**Caraway** (*Carum carvi*): a delicate, leafy plant with dainty white flowers that attract bees and butterflies

**Chives** (*Allium schoenoprasum*): attractive, bluey-purple pom-pom flowers that attract bees and butterflies

**Fennel** (*Foeniculum vulgare*): feathery foliage with striking yellow flowers that attract hoverflies. Birds feed on seeds, and it provides food for butterfly larvae

**Lavender** (*Lavandula species*): fragrant purple flowers attract bees and butterflies in great numbers

**Lemon balm** (*Melissa officinalis*): pale yellow flowers that attract birds, bees, and other insects

**Mint** (*Mentha spicata*): aromatic pink or white flowers that attract bees and butterflies

**Oregano** (*Origanum vulgare*): small white flowers attract bees and butterflies

**Rosemary** (*Rosmarinus officinalis*): pale blue flowers attract lots of bees

**Sage** (*Salvia officinalis*): blue flowers attract bees and butterflies

**Thyme** (*Thymus* species): low growing with pale pink flowers that attract bees and butterflies

ABOVE (LEFT TO RIGHT)
*Cilantro (coriander) is a very popular herb, is easy to grow, and its flowers are particularly useful in the wildlife garden; chamomile is such a pretty herb that it can be grown in containers for decorative effect as well as for its herbal uses; when left to go to flower, chives will attract bees into the garden.*

RIGHT (LEFT TO RIGHT) *Planting a mixture of fruit and herbs in a container will attract a range of insects; lovage is a useful herb in the kitchen that attracts insects, too; lavender is a beautiful plant which flowers throughout summer and is loved by bees among other insects.*

# Companion planting

*Companion planting works on the principle that putting specific plants together will help to reduce attacks from predators on one or other of the plants, attract beneficial insects, and provide helpful nutrients and conditions that will benefit one or both of the plants. It has been practiced around the world for hundreds of years, and works as a simple and effective pest control and natural way to improve the health and yield of fruit and vegetable crops.*

Creating a natural balance in the garden is especially important when gardening organically, and companion planting encourages this, helping to provide pest control without the need for artificial chemicals.

Some gardeners are sceptical about companion planting because many of the theories involved are scientifically unproven, but I have found many of the planting combinations to be very useful in my own garden. I have planted basil and marigolds with tomatoes for many years and, without a doubt, planting nasturtiums helps to reduce aphid attacks on various vegetable crops.

Beans and sweet peas look lovely climbing twiggy wigwams together and the beans have definitely produced a more abundant crop than when planted elsewhere in the garden, perhaps helped by the increase in pollinating insects. Obviously, there may have been other factors involved in these successes, but companion planting is easy to do, costs nothing, and is surely worth a try.

# What to plant

Below is a list of plants, fruits, and vegetables that are particularly beneficial to each crop. Some, such as marigolds and nasturtiums, are all-round good choices because they are suitable for planting just about anywhere in the vegetable garden and help to reduce attacks by predators. The plants and herbs will all provide pest control by deterring insects with their scent or by acting as a sacrificial host plant to attract predators, leaving the crops free from attack.

Vegetable and fruit companions will give you ideas for crops to grow together, providing valuable nutrients and chemicals to benefit plants which will in turn produce healthier plants that are more resistant to pests.

## Vegetables

**Asparagus:** grow with basil, parsley, dill, cilantro (coriander), French marigolds (*Tagetes* species), and tomatoes.

**Aubergines:** see eggplant

**Basil:** can improve the vigor of asparagus, while parsley can improve the flavor. Dill, cilantro (coriander), and marigolds will help to deter aphids and tomatoes will deter asparagus beetle.

**Beets (beetroot):** grow with French marigolds. The marigolds will attract hoverflies which will eat aphids.

**Brassica** (cabbages, cauliflowers, broccoli, etc): grow with nasturtiums (*Tropaeolum majus*), French marigolds, mint, sage, rosemary and dill. Nasturtiums act as a host for cabbage white butterflies, which are also deterred by the smell of marigolds and sage. Mint helps to deter flea beetles. Rosemary can help to repel cabbage fly, and dill attracts wasps that will feast on cabbage worms and may improve growth and flavor.

**Broad beans:** see fava beans

**Carrots:** grow with onions, garlic, leeks, cilantro (coriander), rosemary, chives, lavender, sage, mint, and parsley. All these will overpower the scent of carrots, confusing the carrot fly so that it will not attack crops.

**Celery:** grow with leeks, chives, and garlic. All three will improve the growth and vigor of crops and deter aphids.

**Courgettes:** see zucchini

**Cucumbers:** grow with radishes to deter cucumber beetles.

OPPOSITE *French marigolds planted with tomatoes will help to repel white fly, leaving a healthy crop of fruit.*

ABOVE *The pretty purple flowers of eggplant (aubergine). Planting French marigolds and basil with them will help to protect the crops from white fly infestations.*

**Eggplant (aubergines):** grow with French marigolds and basil. Basil will play host to white fly and so protect the eggplant. Marigolds will repel white fly and may deter nematodes.

**Fava beans (broad beans):** grow with summer savory (*Satureja hortensis*) and poached egg plant (*Limnanthes douglasii*). Summer savory repels black fly with its odor, while the poached egg plant attracts hoverflies and ladybugs, which will eat aphids.

**French beans:** grow with rosemary, sage, and sweetcorn. Rosemary and sage help to protect against bean beetles, while sweetcorn protects against wind and provides support for beans to climb up.

**Leeks:** grow with lavender (*Lavandula* species) and carrots. The smell of lavender confuses pests and can deter aphids. Carrots deter leek moth.

**Lettuce:** grow with onions, chives, and garlic. All three can help to deter slugs and their pungent smells protect against black fly.

**Onions:** grow with mint and chamomile. Mint confuses onion fly, chamomile improves flavor.

**Peas:** grow with mint and chives. Mint will improve the flavor of the peas and the chives will deter aphids with their scent.

**Peppers:** grow with French marigolds, which will repel white fly.

**Potatoes:** grow with fava beans (broad beans). The beans give cover during frosts, protecting the potatoes and adding nitrogen to the soil, which will benefit the crops.

ABOVE *Planting sage with vegetables can be very beneficial, especially for cabbages and carrots, because the sage will deter both cabbage moth and carrot fly.*

BELOW *Help to protect radish plants from attack by planting mint and nasturtiums next to them.*

**Radish:** grow with mint and nasturtiums. The odor of the mint should deter flea beetles and the nasturtiums will protect against aphids.

**Runner beans:** grow with sweet peas and nasturtiums. Both sweet peas and nasturtiums attract pollinators and so should help increase the runner bean crops as well as playing host to aphids and protecting the beans.

**Spinach:** grow with radish. Leaf miners are attracted to radish leaves rather than to spinach.

**Squash:** grow with borage, French marigolds, nasturtiums, and beans. Borage improves flavor. Marigolds will deter beetles and nasturtiums will deter aphids. Beans will add nitrogen to the soil.

**Sweetcorn:** grow with peas and beans. Both peas and beans add nitrogen to the soil, which helps crops of corn.

**Tomatoes:** grow with nasturtiums, French marigolds, basil, garlic, chives, borage, onion, and asparagus. Grow with marigolds, chives, and garlic to repel white and black fly. Nasturtiums and basil attract aphids, which will protect the tomatoes. Borage will help to protect against tomato hornworm and improve growth and flavor. Basil has the added benefit that it can also improve the taste of the tomatoes.

**Zucchini (courgettes):** grow with English marigolds (*Calendula officinalis*) and flowering herbs, such as thyme and oregano. Flowers attract pollinating insects, which will increase crops.

BELOW *Carrot crops may benefit from being planted with other strong-smelling vegetables such as onions and garlic, which can help to mask the scent of the carrots, protecting them from carrot flies.*

## Fruit

**Apples:** grow with nasturtiums (*Tropaeolum majus*), onions, and chives. The nasturtiums repel codling moths, while onions and chives help to prevent apple scab.

**Blackberries:** grow with tansy, which helps to repel predators.

**Fruit trees (general):** grow with chives, nasturtiums, peas, and beans. All these will discourage predators from climbing up trees because they will be repelled by their odor. Nasturtiums planted around the base of a fruit tree provide a host for aphids. Peas and beans add nitrogen to the soil.

**Gooseberries:** grow with French marigolds (*Tagetes* species) which will deter aphids. However, gooseberries are banned in some US states so do check local regulations.

**Grapes:** grow with chives and basil. Chives will repel aphids and basil will act as a host for aphids.

**Raspberries:** grow with garlic, which repels aphids with its odor.

**Soft fruits (general):** grow with poached egg plant (*Limnanthes douglasii*). The flowers of the poached egg plants will attract insects that will pollinate bushes and also feast on predators.

**Strawberries:** grow with borage and onions. Both improve the flavor of strawberries and help to strengthen plants, while onions can help to prevent mold on the fruit.

ABOVE *Plum trees are almost worth growing for their beautiful pink blossom alone, but the fruits that develop will supply you with a wonderful crop of plums and help to feed visiting birds as well.*

RIGHT *Bergamot flowers attract bees to the garden and can protect roses when they are planted together.*

OPPOSITE *Thyme is an effective companion plant as well as having many culinary uses.*

## Herbs

**Basil:** grow with asparagus, eggplants (aubergines), grapes, tomatoes.

**Bay leaves:** grow with beans.

**Borage:** grow with cabbages, squash, strawberries, tomatoes.

**Chamomile:** grow with cabbages, onions.

**Chives:** grow with carrots, celery, fruit trees, grapes, lettuce, peas, roses, tomatoes.

**Cilantro (coriander):** grow with asparagus.

**Dill:** grow with asparagus, cabbages, lettuce.

**Feverfew:** grow with bergamot (*Monarda* species), roses.

**Hyssop:** grow with cabbages.

**Lavender:** grow with carrots, leeks.

**Mint:** grow with cabbages, carrots, onions, peas, radish, tomatoes.

**Oregano:** grow with brassicas.

**Parsley:** grow with asparagus, carrots, chives, roses.

**Rosemary:** grow with beans, cabbages, carrots.

**Sage:** grow with cabbages, carrots, French beans, tomatoes.

**Summer savory:** grow with fava beans (broad beans).

**Thyme:** grow with cabbages, roses, tomatoes.

## Companion plants for general use

Try the following plants in any areas to keep insects away from other plants that you want to protect.

**Chamomile** (*Chamaemelum nobile*): attracts hoverflies and wasps that feed on predatory insects.

**Geraniums** (scented) (*Pelargonium* species): deter insects from roses, tomatoes, and grapes when planted nearby.

**Marigolds** (*Calendula officinalis* and *Tagetes* species): are a great insect repellent throughout the garden and attract beneficial pollinating insects.

**Morning glory** (*Convolvulus* species): attracts pollinating insects into the garden.

**Nasturtiums** (*Tropaeolum majus*): an attractive host for aphids, preventing attacks on many crops.

**Nettles:** attract cabbage white butterflies, preventing attacks on many crops.

**Poached egg plants** (*Limnanthes douglasii*): attract ladybugs, bees, butterflies, and wasps.

## Flowers that benefit from companion planting

The following plants will benefit from having certain companion plants grown near them.

**Chrysanthemums:** chives deter aphids and encourage pollinating insects.

**Roses:** mint, chives, thyme, garlic, parsley, French marigolds (*Tagetes* species), and English or pot marigolds (*Calendula* species) all help to deter aphids. In particular, the marigolds attract hoverflies, which feast on aphids. The older varieties will encourage pollinating insects into the garden.

**Sunflowers:** chives (same reason as above).

OPPOSITE *Dill flowers are very attractive to the larvae of harlequin ladybugs.*

ABOVE *Nasturtiums will continue to flower throughout the summer months, acting as valuable companion plants and bringing a blast of color to the garden.*

LEFT *Roses can be prone to attack by aphids, but planting strong smelling plants around them can help to keep them free from attack.*

# CHAPTER NINE

# Container gardening

Growing plants in containers is a very practical approach to gardening because it offers valuable growing opportunities for even the tiniest of spaces. From the humblest window box, bursting with flowers that attract pollinators to your windowsill, to collections of old sinks, water troughs, and bathtubs for shrubs and climbing plants, containers can suit any garden or backyard, big or small.

Many different plants can be grown in containers, from flowering annuals that will add a splash of color to your garden for one season to more long-term planting, including climbers and shrubs that will stay in place for years. For any container planting, it is important to provide the correct conditions for the plants, ensuring that there are drainage holes, using nutrient-rich compost and soil, and adding moisture-retaining granules or sand and grit to lighten the soil. This is especially important for shrubs and perennial plants. Containers are a great way of creating a garden when you do not have much outside space, and are also useful in larger, more established gardens.

# The benefits *of* container gardening

*One of the benefits of gardening in pots is that plants which require different growing conditions can be displayed and arranged together, each container providing for its individual plant. A mini wildflower garden in a pot, which favors relatively poor soil, can sit next to a potted rose that thrives in rich, fertile compost.*

It's a great way to grow some varieties of fruit and vegetables because they, too, often have very specific nutritional needs. Many crops thrive when grown in containers, and they are perfect for gardeners who have only a balcony or roof terrace but want to cultivate their own food.

In the wildlife garden, pots are very useful because they can be planted with insect-attracting plants (such as nettles, weeds, and grasses) that you might not want to plant directly into the ground, and can be then dotted around the garden and nestled into borders.

Grouping containers together can also create the effect of a border—even on a patio or in a courtyard garden—and can encourage and provide food for a whole host of wildlife without the need for a garden at all.

## Choosing a container

Just about any container can be used as long as it has a few drainage holes and enough room for plant roots to grow. I have been buying old buckets and enamel pans from car-boot sales for

LEFT *Salad crops grow well in containers, making them suitable for balconies and small gardens. Position them near the back door for easy access.*

OPPOSITE *Plant basil seeds in pots and carefully transplant the seedlings when they are large enough to handle.*

years and have now amassed quite a collection, spending only a small amount on each one. I love the rather hodgepodge look of them all grouped together. Look out for old food cans, enamel breadbins, and even old galvanized washtubs, which can all be put to good use and are a great way to recycle, or visit garden centers for elegant terracotta pots and tubs if your garden is more formal.

## Planting a container

When you have chosen your container, you are then ready to plant it.

**1** Make sure that it is clean and has a few drainage holes in the bottom. If you need to add some, use a drill or hammer and make holes with a heavy-duty nail.

**2** Soak your plants' roots for about 20 minutes by standing them in a bucket or bowl of water.

**3** Cover the container's drainage holes with broken pieces of plant pot (this allows water to drain away, but helps to prevent any soil from leaching out with it). Add quite a few if you are using a large container.

**4** Fill the container about two-thirds full with potting compost. If your container is small, add some water-retaining granules (following the manufacturer's instructions) to help prevent the potting compost from drying out in warm weather.

**5** For large containers, add a few handfuls of perlite to the soil to lighten the compost and improve drainage.

**6** If your plant is to stay in its container permanently (rather than for a few months over the summer, for example), then add some slow-release fertilizer (available from garden centers) to the potting compost to help the plant stay healthy.

**7** Take each plant out of its pot and place it in the container. The surface of each plant's compost should be about 1¼in (3cm) below the rim. Add or take away potting compost as necessary.

## A weighty matter

If you decide to use large tubs on a balcony or roof terrace, bear in mind the weight of the containers and ensure that they will not cause damage to your building.

**8** Fill in the gaps around the plants with potting compost, pressing down gently to get rid of any air pockets. Firm down the surface and water well.

## Feeding and deadheading container plants

The potting compost used for your containers should contain enough nutrients for small plants for the first few weeks. After that, use a liquid feed every couple of weeks, such as diluted wormery liquid (see page 36) or seaweed feed to keep the plants in good condition. Deadhead the plants regularly to encourage continual flowering, and remove any straggly stems and leaves.

## Moisture

It's very important to keep containers moist, so regular watering is vital, especially in hot, dry weather. If you are unable to water them for a few days, stand the pots in dishes or bowls to conserve moisture and group them together in a shady spot to prevent them drying out too much.

OPPOSITE *Mint can become very invasive when planted in a border, so growing it in pots will give you a plentiful supply but keep it in check.*

# Plant a bee-friendly container

For a bee-friendly container that will flower throughout the summer, choose a range of plants to attract as many bees as possible.

If possible, select a large tub so that you can pack in as many nectar- and pollen-rich plants as you can. Prepare the tub following the instructions on page 131, and try some of the following plants:

**Common Mint or Spearmint** (*Mentha spicata*): flowers in summer

**Foxglove** (*Digitalis* species): flowers from late spring to midsummer

**Globe Thistle** (*Echinops* species): flowers from early summer onward

**Ice Plant** (*Sedum spectabile*): flowers from summer through to fall

**Lavender** (*Lavandula* species): flowers in summer

**Macedonian Scabious** (*Knautia macedonica*): flowers from early summer

**Meadow Cranesbill** (*Geranium pratense*): flowers in early summer

**Purple Coneflower** (*Echinacea purpurea*): flowers from summer through to fall

**Teasel** (*Dipsacus fullonum*): flowers in summer through to fall

**Thyme** (*Thymus vulgaris*): flowers from spring through to fall

LEFT *Grouping several lavender plants together in a tub will create a treat for bees and butterflies.*

# MAKE A BEE-FRIENDLY HERB TUB

Make a bee-friendly pot that will provide beautiful herbs for the kitchen as well. Here, an old metal wok has been repurposed to make an attractive planter that is perfect for a collection of fragrant thyme plants that will captivate any number of bees and butterflies. Thyme is quite low-growing and does not need deep soil, so this container works well.

## YOU WILL NEED

**Large metal wok (or a similar shallow pan)**

**Gravel**

**Sand**

**Potting compost**

**A varied selection of thyme plants**

1 Drill holes in the base of the wok for drainage, and add enough gravel to cover the base of the wok as thyme likes very well-drained soil.

2 Mix a few handfuls of sand with the potting compost to mimic the soil that thyme would naturally grow in. Pour the sand and potting compost mixture into the wok and spread it out.

3 Soak the thyme plants in water so that the roots are thoroughly wet and take them out of their pots.

4 Gently pull the roots out to encourage them to spread in their new surroundings, and plant them in the wok, scooping holes in the potting compost and pushing the plants into them.

5 If necessary, add more potting compost to even the surface, and flatten it off.

6 Place some gravel and a few larger stones over the surface of the potting compost. This gives a decorative touch, but it will also help to retain moisture and heat.

# Plant a butterfly container

Butterflies are attracted by color, so planting a range of flowers in pinks, oranges, reds, yellows, and purples in one container will provide plenty of nectar and hopefully appeal to lots of different butterflies. Planting nettles, thistles, and nasturtiums nearby may also encourage butterflies to breed by providing food for butterfly larvae.

Try some of the following plants:

**Argentinian Vervain** (*Verbena bonariensis*): flowers in summer
**Astrantia** or **Masterwort** (*Astrantia major*): flowers in summer
**Buddleja** or **Buddleia** (*Buddleja* species): new dwarf varieties are now available, and are perfect for containers; flowers from summer to fall
**Cornflower** (*Centaurea cyanus*): flowers from summer
**Honesty** (*Lunaria annua*): flowers from early summer
**Ice Plant** (*Sedum spectabile*): flowers from summer to fall
**Lavender** (*Lavandula* species): flowers in summer
**Marigold** (*Calendula officinalis*): flowers from early summer
**Marjoram** (*Origanum vulgare*): flowers in summer
**Zinnia** (*Zinnia elegans*): flowers from summer

# Plant a tub for moths

Like butterflies, moth populations are in decline and they are often overlooked in a wildlife garden, possibly because they are often seen as a little dull and less striking than other insects. In fact, moths can be quite beautiful and very colorful. They are a vitally important part of our ecosystem, and we should do all we can to protect them and help to increase numbers.

Providing caterpillar food plants in your garden can encourage moths to breed, which will in turn benefit birds, frogs, toads, bats, and hedgehogs among other creatures that feed on the caterpillars. Moths are important pollinators in the garden and are attracted to nectar-rich flowers. They are most active in the evening and are drawn to light-colored flowers, so providing a range of night-scented plants will encourage them into your garden.

To create a moth-friendly pot that will flower over the summer and into fall, follow the instructions on page 131 and pot up your container with a selection of the following:

**Common Knapweed** (*Centaurea nigra*): flowers in summer

**Evening Primrose** (*Oenothera biennis*): flowers from summer right through to fall

**Globe Artichoke** (*Cynara cardunculus*): flowers from early summer through to fall

**Ice Plant** (*Sedum spectabile*): flowers from summer through to fall

**Night-scented Stock** (*Matthiola longipetala*): flowers in summer

**Red Valerian** (*Centranthus ruber*): flowers from spring through to fall

**Sea Holly** (*Eryngium giganteum*): flowers in summer

**Small Scabious** (*Scabiosa columbaria*): flowers from summer through to fall

**Sweet Rocket** (*Hesperis matronalis*): flowers from early summer

**Winged Tobacco** (*Nicotiana alata*): flowers in summer

ABOVE Nicotiana, *with its fragranced white flowers blooms throughout the summer and attracts moths into the garden.*

# Growing fruit *and* vegetables *in* containers

*Many wildlife-friendly fruits and vegetables are well suited to container gardening, which is great news for those with small gardens and backyards, balconies, roof-top gardens, or even just a windowsill.*

Fruits in particular are perfect for growing in pots, especially strawberry plants and currant bushes. Even fruit trees, such as apple, pear, and peach, can all do well in containers, with dwarf varieties being perfect for the conditions.

When growing fruit and vegetables in pots, it is important to provide a suitable growing medium for each crop and to feed and water them regularly to ensure healthy growth. If your space is limited, choose your crops carefully so that you can enjoy the twin benefits of eating delicious home-grown crops and the pleasure of seeing butterflies, bees, and other insects up close. For further information, see Chapter 8.

LEFT *Fruit can be grown in lots of different containers, but this sturdy wooden box is particularly effective because several plants can be grown at once, thus producing a plentiful supply of strawberries.*

# PLANT A MINIATURE FRUIT AND VEGETABLE GARDEN

This miniature wildlife garden in a trug contains plants that are all wildlife friendly and which benefit one another well. Alpine strawberries, cherry tomatoes, marigolds (*Calendula officinalis*), and a sunflower (*Helianthus annuus*) sit along side a few herbs, such as basil, that are appealing to bees and butterflies and look very pretty together.

## YOU WILL NEED

**Metal trug or basket**

**Drainage crocks**

**Gravel**

**Potting compost**

**Moisture-retaining granules**

**Sunflower** (*Helianthus annuus*)

**Alpine strawberry** (*Fragaria vesca*)

**Cherry tomato** (*Lycopersicon esculentum*)

**Pot marigold** (*Calendula officinalis*)

**Purple basil** (*Ocimum basilicum* var. *purpurascens*)

1 Make holes in the base of the trug or basket with a drill or a hammer and nail.

2 Cover the holes with broken pots and add a few handfuls of gravel in the bottom to aid drainage.

3 Put some potting compost into the trug, adding a few handfuls of moisture-retaining granules, which will help to prevent the trug from drying out.

4 Soak all the plants well, and then carefully take them out of their pots.

5 Position the sunflower at the back of the trug. Then put the other plants in the trug, placing the alpine strawberries around the front so that they spill over the edge.

6 Fill the trug with potting compost and firm it down gently around each plant. Water well and feed with natural fertilizer every week.

# Resources

Great sources of information on wildlife, conservation, and horticulture.

## UK WEBSITES

**British Beekeepers Association**
bbka.org.uk

**BBC Gardening**
bbc.co.uk/gardening

**Bumblebee Conservation Trust**
bumblebeeconservation.org

**British Hedgehog Preservation Society**
britishhedgehogs.org.uk

**British Trust for Ornithology**
bto.org

**Buglife**
buglife.org.uk

**Butterfly Conservation**
butterfly-conservation.org

**Froglife**
froglife.org

**Hedgehog Street**
hedgehogstreet.org

**London Wildlife Trust**
wildlondon.org.uk

**Natural England**
naturalengland.org.uk

**Royal Horticultural Society**
rhs.org.uk

**RSPB**
rspb.org.uk

**The Wildlife Trust**
wildlifetrusts.org

**Wild About Gardens**
wildaboutgardens.org.uk

**Wildlife Gardening**
wildlifegardening.co.uk

**Wildlife Garden Project**
wildlifegardenproject.com

**World Wildlife Fund**
wwf.org.uk

## WILDLIFE GARDENING SUPPLIES

**Ark Wildlife Supplies**
arkwildlife.co.uk

**Chiltern Seeds**
chilternseeds.co.uk

**Habitat Aid**
habitataid.co.uk

**Lilies Water Gardens**
lilieswatergardens.co.uk

**Really Wild Flowers**
reallywildflowers.co.uk

**RSPB**
shopping.rspb.org.uk

**Sarah Raven**
sarahraven.com

**Suttons seeds**
suttons.co.uk

**Wiggly Wigglers**
wigglywigglers.co.uk

**Wildflower Shop**
wildflower.org.uk

## US WEBSITES

**All About Wildlife**
allaboutwildlife.com

**American Beekeepers Federation**
abfnet.org

**American Bird Conservancy**
abcbirds.org

**Beautiful Wildlife Garden**
beautifulwildlifegarden.com

**Buzz About Bees**
buzzaboutbees.net

**Garden Mandy**
gardenmandy.com

**Garden Simply**
gardensimply.com

**National Wildlife Federation**
nwf.org

**Native Plants and Wildlife**
nativeplantwildlifegarden.com

**North American Butterfly Association**
naba.org

**The Organic Gardener**
the-organic-gardener.com

**The Xerces Society**
xerces.org

## WILDLIFE GARDENING SUPPLIES

**American Meadows**
americanmeadows.com

**Green Roof Plants**
greenroofplants.com

**Hancock Seed Company**
hancockseed.com

**Prairie Nursery**
prairienursery.com

**Seeds of Change**
seedsofchange.com

**Wild Birds Unlimited**
wbu.com

**Wildflower Mix**
wildflowermix.com

# Index

# Acknowledgments

My heartfelt thanks go to Vanessa Daubney for such thoughtful editing, Sarah Rock for creating the look of the book so well, Debbie Patterson for the beautiful additional photography and for amazing patience when photographing wildlife, Alexandra Campbell for sourcing great locations, and particularly to The Abbey Physic Community Garden, Faversham, Kent (a charity offering horticultural training, a wildlife-friendly environment, and support for adults with problems such as bereavement, mental health issues, or physical disabilities, www.abbeyphysiccommunitygarden.org), Frances Beaumont Dip COT, Cert Ed (Frances opens her garden for Dyspraxia Action, www.dyspraxia-action.org), and Ian and Moe Parker (who make bird, bat, and bug boxes for the wildlife park at Oare Gunpowder Works, Faversham, Kent, www.gunpowderworks.co.uk) for generously allowing us to photograph their inspirational wildlife gardens.

Thank you to Cindy Richards of CICO Books who, once again, has given me a fantastic opportunity for which I am very grateful. Thank you and all my love to Laurie, Gracie, and Betty for many reasons, all much appreciated. And last but by no means least, thank you to Gillian Haslam, editor extraordinaire, for patience in the extreme, much valued guidance, and support throughout. We got there in the end! Thank you all.

# Photography credits

All photos copyright CICO Books, unless otherwise stated.

Earth background photo © goclaygo/istockphoto.com; page 1: Mark Lohman; page 2: Raimund Koch-View/Alamy Stock Photo; page 3: Caroline Hughes; page 4: Debbie Patterson; page 5, top: Debbie Patterson, bottom: Jonathan Buckley; page 6: Debbie Patterson; page 7: Caroline Arber; page 8: Debbie Patterson; page 10: Debbie Patterson; page 11: Debbie Patterson; page 12: Amanda Darcy; page 13: Debbie Patterson; page 14: Tracy Litterick; page 15: Debbie Patterson; page 17: Simon Brown; page 18: Rachel Whiting; page 20: David Merewether; page 21: David Merewether; page 22, top: Polly Wreford, bottom: Heini Schneebeli; page 23: Polly Wreford; page 24: Debbie Patterson; page 25: Mark Lohman; page 26: Hervé Roncière; page 27, top: Hervé Roncière; page 27, bottom: David Merewether; page 28: Debbie Patterson; page 29: Polly Wreford; page 30: Alan Williams; page 31: Debbie Patterson; page 32: Debbie Patterson; page 33: Anne Hyde; page 34: Hervé Roncière; page 35: Debbie Patterson; page 37: Debbie Patterson; page 38: Debbie Patterson; page 40: Debbie Patterson; page 41: Pete Moore; page 42: Debbie Patterson; page 43: Pete Moore; page 44: Debbie Patterson; page 46: Debbie Patterson; page 47: Debbie Patterson; page 48: Caroline Hughes; page 49: Debbie Patterson; page 50: Andrea Jones; page 51: Debbie Patterson; page 52: Debbie Patterson; page 54: Debbie Patterson; page 55: Debbie Patterson; page 56: Debbie Patterson; page 57: Debbie Patterson; page 58: Francesca Yorke; page 59: Amanda Darcy; page 61: Debbie Patterson; page 62: Mark Lohman; page 63: © C J M McKendry/istockphoto.com; page 64: Caroline Arber; page 66: Caroline Arber; page 67: Caroline Arber; page 68: Debbie Patterson; page 70: Polly Wreford; page 71: Polly Wreford; page 72: Holly Jolliffe; page 73, top and bottom: Caroline Arber; page 74, top: Holly Jolliffe, bottom: Polly Wreford; page 75: Debbie Patterson; page 76: Polly Wreford; page 77: Debbie Patterson; page 78: Debbie Patterson; page 80: Mark Lohman; page 81: David Merewether; page 82: Heini Schneebeli; page 83 © Tom Gowanlock/Shutterstock; page 84: David Merewether; page 85, top: David Merewether, bottom: Glyn Thomas/Alamy Stock Photo; page 86: Debbie Patterson; page 88: Debbie Patterson; page 89: Debbie Patterson; page 90: Debbie Patterson; page 91: Amanda Darcy; page 92: Debbie Patterson; page 93: Debbie Patterson; page 94: Debbie Patterson; page 95: Debbie Patterson; page 96: Debbie Patterson; page 97: Debbie Patterson; page 98: Andrea Jones; page 99: Andrea Jones; page 100: Debbie Patterson; page 102, left and right: Mark Lohman; page 103: Amanda Darcy; page 104: Polly Wreford; page 105: Amanda Darcy; page 106: Carolyn Barber; page 107, top left: Emma Mitchell, top left and bottom: Debbie Patterson; page 108: David Merewether; page 110: David Merewether; page 111: Heini Schneebeli; page 112: David Merewether; page 113: Caroline Hughes; page 114: Debbie Patterson; page 116, top left: Heini Schneebeli, top right: Caroline Hughes, bottom: Keiko Oikawa; page 117, top: David Merewether, bottom left: Caroline Arber, bottom right: Debbie Patterson; page 118: Heini Schneebeli; page 119: Debbie Patterson; page 120, top: David Merewether, bottom: Caroline Hughes; page 121: Amanda Darcy; page 122, top: David Merewether, bottom: Caroline Hughes; page 123: Heini Schneebeli; page 124: Caroline Hughes; page 125, top and bottom: Debbie Patterson; page 126: Heini Schneebeli; page 128: Debbie Patterson; page 129: David Merewether; page 130: Heini Schneebeli; page 132: Debbie Patterson; page 133, top and bottom: Caroline Hughes; page 134, left: David Merewether, right: Debbie Patterson; page 135: Debbie Patterson; page 136: Polly Wreford; page 137: Debbie Patterson.